ISBN 978-1-334-78807-9
PIBN 10655531

This book is a reproduction of an important historical work. Forgotten Books uses
state-of-the-art technology to digitally reconstruct the work, preserving the original format
whilst repairing imperfections present in the aged copy. In rare cases, an imperfection in
the original, such as a blemish or missing page, may be replicated in our edition. We do,
however, repair the vast majority of imperfections successfully; any imperfections that
remain are intentionally left to preserve the state of such historical works.

English
Français
Deutsche
Italiano
Español
Português

www.forgottenbooks.com

Mythology Photography **Fiction**
Fishing Christianity **Art** Cooking
Essays Buddhism Freemasonry
Medicine **Biology** Music **Ancient**
Egypt Evolution Carpentry Physics
Dance Geology **Mathematics** Fitness
Shakespeare **Folklore** Yoga Marketing
Confidence Immortality Biographies
Poetry **Psychology** Witchcraft
Electronics Chemistry History **Law**
Accounting **Philosophy** Anthropology
Alchemy Drama Quantum Mechanics
Atheism Sexual Health **Ancient History**
Entrepreneurship Languages Sport
Paleontology Needlework Islam
Metaphysics Investment Archaeology
Parenting Statistics Criminology
Motivational

LETTERS

FROM

GEORGE LORD CAREW

TO

SIR THOMAS ROE,

AMBASSADOR TO THE COURT OF THE GREAT MOGUL.

1615—1617.

EDITED BY

JOHN MACLEAN, F.S.A.

ETC. ETC.

KEEPER OF THE RECORDS OF H.M. ORDNANCE IN THE TOWER OF LONDON,
EDITOR OF THE LIFE OF SIR PETER CAREW, KNT.

WESTMINSTER:

J. B. NICHOLS AND SONS, PRINTERS,

PARLIAMENT STREET.

[LXXVI.]

PREFACE.

THE Members of the Camden Society are indebted to Mrs. Everett Green for the publication of the interesting letters printed on the following pages. In pursuing her labours at the State Paper Office, the valuable fruits of which we have received in four rich volumes, she discovered these documents, and brought them into the series of Domestic Correspondence from the various incongruous places in which they were deposited, and, knowing that I am engaged in preparing a memoir of the writer, she kindly introduced them to my notice. Of Lord Carew himself, however, they afford very scanty information. It is not a little singular that in relating all the gossip, both public and private, he could from day to day collect, he mentions himself, directly, once only. This was on the occasion of his being sworn a Member of the Privy Council, and, in communicating the event to his friend, with the marked humility frequently observed in men of such eminence, he requests his prayers, in the words of the Litany, "that it may please God to send him grace, wisdom, and understanding." If however in this particular the letters are deficient,

they throw very considerable light upon the period to
which they relate, and reveal to us numerous facts and
the dates of many events not elsewhere found.

In England, fortunately, during this period no very
exciting transactions occurred, if we except the murder
of Sir Thomas Overbury, which caused no little stir.
The events which took place abroad, however, were of
greater interest as affecting the world at large. In
France the jealousies of the royal family, superadded to
the religious dissensions which prevailed, rent the country
from the English Channel to the Mediterranean Sea, and
led to a war in which the King was arrayed against
the Princes and the Princes against the King. The
sacrifice of the life of the Marshal d'Ancre by order of
Louis partially healed the quarrel, but it soon broke out
again with increased fury, and led to a civil war, which
was only quelled after an enormous expenditure of blood
and treasure. Italy, as usual, was a battle-field. The
plains of Piedmont and Milan were wasted by war in
consequence of the struggles of the houses of Austria
and Savoy for the possession of Monferrat. In the
Netherlands great distractions prevailed on account of
religious differences between the Protestant sects, especially the Lutherans and Calvinists, who hated each other
little less than they hated the Pope. Upon all these
matters the Lord Carew seems to have been exceedingly
well informed, and he communicated to his friend the
intelligence he possessed with very little reserve, con-

sidering the habitual caution of an experienced courtier of the reign of Queen Elizabeth. This caution is manifested in several places by a request that his letters may be burnt, and in his last communication this request is reiterated in a postscript, to the effect that they might be so destroyed or returned to him. Fortunately, as is usual in such cases, the request was disregarded, and the letters are preserved to us.

Upon perusing these letters and observing the great historical interest which they possess, I considered them well worth publication, and, having submitted them to the Council of the Camden Society with an offer to edit them for the Society, the Council was pleased to accept my proposal. In the execution of this trust I have endeavoured to adhere as closely as possible to the original orthography, except that, in accordance with the practice of the Society, words which in the original are contracted are printed in full. I have further added such foot-notes as appeared to be desirable in illustration of the text. In preparing the Index, where a name occurs more than once on the same page I have not repeated the reference.

As the papers have been prepared for the press in the intervals of business of an engrossing nature, I am conscious that several errors will be noticed by the reader. In respect to such I must bespeak his favourable indulgence.

Having said thus much of the letters, I will add a few words respecting the writer and the person to whom they were addressed. Both these men were too eminent in their own day and are too well known in ours to require much to be written concerning them.

GEORGE LORD CAREW was the second son of Dr. George Carew, who held the deanery of Windsor and other preferments in the reign of Queen Elizabeth. He was born in 1557, and entered the University of Oxford in 1572, but left without taking a degree. He distinguished himself at an early age in the Irish wars, and in 1585 received the honour of knighthood from the Lord Deputy. Having written a treatise on the condition of Ireland, which showed a consummate knowledge of the state of the country, the Queen, when the whole of Ireland was in a state of revolt after the failure of the expedition of the Earl of Essex, made choice of him as Lord President of Munster. His conduct in this office fully justified her Majesty's confidence in his integrity, capacity, and judgment; for the suppression of the rebellion was chiefly owing to his valour in the field and his wisdom in the council. By James I. he was no less esteemed. On the accession of that monarch he was created Baron Carew of Clopton, and made Vice-Chamberlain to the Queen and Receiver-General of her revenues. Moreover, on the death of the Earl of Devonshire the office of Master of the Ordnance was granted to him for life. He held these offices at the date of this correspondence; and, being constantly resident at Court, he was well informed on all passing subjects of interest.

After the death of Queen Anne he became Chamberlain
to the Prince of Wales, whose good graces also he
secured.   On the Prince's accession to the throne he
was advanced, for his long and meritorious services, to
the dignity of Earl of Totnes.   He died at his house in
the Savoy 1629.   Lord Carew was a man of learning and
ability, and was much attached to antiquarian pursuits,
particularly genealogy.   There are in the Lambeth library
numerous valuable pedigrees, generally of Irish families,
in his hand-writing.   He was an intimate friend of
Camden, whom he assisted in preparing the " Britannia."

Sir Thomas Roe was no less eminent as a diplomatist
than the Lord Carew as a soldier.   He was descended
from a family originally seated in Kent, and was the son
of Robert Roe, of Lower Layton, Essex, and grandson of
Sir Thomas Roe, Lord Mayor of London in 1568.   He was
born about 1580, and studied at Magdalen College, Oxford, but left without attaining his degree.   He received
the honour of knighthood in 1604, but his first public
employment of importance was his mission to the Great
Mogul in 1614, on which occasion these letters were
written.   The object of this embassy was to promote the
extension of trade in the East, and the expenses were paid
by the East India Company.*   Sir Thomas succeeded most
satisfactorily.   Our Indian empire owes. much to the
treaties which he established, and he gained great and

* S. P. O. Dom. Corr. Jas. I., vol. lxxviii. 61.

deserved credit from his employment. He arrived at
Adsmere, where the Mogul resided, on the 22nd Decem
ber, 1615, and was met, he says, by Mr. Edwards, the
resident agent of the East India Company, "accompanied with the famous unwearied walker, Thomas Co-
ryatt, who on foote had passed most of Europe and Asya,
and was now arrived in India, being but the beginning
of his purposed travells." Roe's original journal of this
embassy is preserved in the British Museum.[a] In it he
gives an interesting account of the Mogul empire, the
customs of the Court, and the manners of the inhabitants. Sir Thomas Roe's next embassy was in 1621,
when he was sent to the Court of Constantinople with
very much the same object as his mission to India. He
remained until 1628; and, by his prudence and sagacity, succeeded in obtaining the most valuable results,
not only for the extension of trade, but even for the
Christian religion itself. His letters and negociations
relating to this embassy were published in 1740 in one
volume folio by Samuel Richardson, the expense being
partially borne by the "Society for the Encouragement
of Learning."[b] This volume was edited by Carte the
historian, from whom there is a very interesting letter
dated 20 March, 1736-7,[c] addressed to the secretary to
the Society, relative to the publication of these and the
rest of Roe's papers, which were all at that time the

---

[a] Addit. MSS. 6115.   [b] Addit. MSS. 6185.   [c] Addit. MSS. 6190. 21.

property of Richardson.[a] It appears that "from the time of his being sent to Constantinople there was a continued series of his letters and negociations till the end of his life." Carte carefully examined the documents, and he gives his opinion as to what portion of them it was desirable to publish, and the manner of such publication. He estimated that, by retrenching letters containing the same accounts, and those of compliments, the work might be embraced in two volumes folio in addition to the Turkish negociations, unless it were determined to print also translations of such letters as were written in German or Italian, of which there were a great number; in which case an additional volume would, he thought, be necessary. The first volume, containing the Turkish negociations, was the only one published.

All the papers appear to have been carefully arranged for publication, but the printing of the second volume was delayed in consequence of Carte's absence from England,[b] and finally abandoned upon the dissolution of the Society in 1749. What has become of these documents is a question of considerable interest. Carte specifically mentions the four letters printed in this volume as being with Roe's papers. He says, "There are also 4 long letters of the Earl of Totnes to him during that embassy, containing a journal of occurrences, as well in England as in other partes of Europe, from

[a] Addit. MSS. 6185. 111.   [b] Addit. MSS. 6185. 103.

1615 to 1617, which, containing short memorials of
facte, like Cambden's summary of King James' Reign,
may by some be thought as curious." As these letters
were found in the State Paper Office it would naturally
be concluded that the bulk of the correspondence would
be discovered there also; and there is, certainly, in that
repository a great mass of Roe's papers, and these were
formerly tied up in separate bundles, but some years
ago were distributed among the various collections to
which they belong, according to the system of arrangement which obtains in the office. It appears from
Carte's letter that he marked many of the papers which
passed through his hands. I have, however, examined
a considerable quantity, and cannot find one letter
bearing any peculiar mark. Many of the documents in
the printed volume are found here, but counterparts
might have been used for publication. There is also a
memorandum in existence which shows that a volume
of Sir Thomas Roe's Correspondence had been lent to the
Earl of Oxford. This volume now forms No. 1901 of the
Harleian Collection in the British Museum, and contains
letters *written by* Sir Thomas Roe only, whilst in the
bundles of the correspondence for the same period letters
to him alone are found. Were it not for the discovery
of Lord Carew's letters in the State Paper Office I should
conclude that Richardson's papers might be still in
private hands; but, if such be the case, how got these
letters among the national archives?

But to return from this digression.

In 1629 Sir Thomas Roe was sent ambassador to Poland and Sweden, and on his way treated with the King of Denmark, as also on his return. Advantage was taken of this occasion to endeavour the reconciliation of the Lutherans and Calvinists, and unite them all in conformity with the Church of England. Although this last matter failed, great advantages to trade and commerce were obtained through his negociations.

In 1641 he was sent ambassador to the emperor and the princes of Germany to be present at the Diet of Ratisbon, and there to mediate on behalf of the Prince Elector Palatine. The Emperor was so pleased with his conduct and his great abilities that he several times said in public: "I have met with many gallant persons of many nations, but I scarce ever met with an ambassador till now." On his return from Germany he was made Chancellor of the Garter and a Privy Councillor, but he lived not long to enjoy these honours. He died 6th November, 1644.

Sir Thomas Roe was undoubtedly a man of great parts—a scholar, a gentleman, and a courtier. Carte, speaking of his letters and papers, says: "I have read them with great pleasure, and cannot sufficiently admire his rare abilities, judgment, and integrity, his extraordinary sagacity in discovering the views and designs of those with whom he treated, and his admirable dexterity in guarding against their measures and bringing them

over to his purpose. Wise, experienced, penetrating,
and knowing, he was never to be surprised or deceived,
and though no minister ever had greater difficulties to
struggle with, or was employed by a Court that had less
power to support him, yet he supported all his employments with dignity, and came out of them with reputation and honour.   In all the honest arts of negociation
he had few equals, (I dare say) no superiors. His
letters and papers are a treasure that ought to be communicated to the world."

J. M.

LETTERS OF GEORGE LORD CAREW.

LETTER I.[a]

My Lord Ambassador:—To geve you testimonie I am nott vn- A.D. 1615. myndfull of my promesse, to lett you know in thatt remote part of the world where you live how thinges passe in these partes, I send you this ensuinge rapsodie of thinges past.   In Januarie last the Earl of January. Kent [b] died; his old brother, to the knees in the grave, livethe, and my Ladie Elizabeth Grey is but yet the Ladie Ruthen.   Sir Moyle Finche [c] is also dead; his wife, pressed with suters, being, as I take itt,

[a] S.P.O. Dom. Corr. vol. lxxx. 85.

[b] Henry Grey, called 7th Earl of Kent.   Richard, the third Earl, having greatly wasted his estate by gaming, died at an inn in Lombard Street.   The right to the Earldom devolved upon his half-brother, Henry Grey, who abstained from assuming the title because he had not sufficient property to maintain its dignity.   His only son, Henry Grey, for the same reason as his father, declined the title, but he left three sons who were successively Earls of Kent: viz., Reginald, who by the exercise of great frugality nearly recovered the paternal estate, and re-assumed the honours of the family.   On his death s.p. in 1572, he was succeeded by the nobleman mentioned in the text, who also died s.p., aged 74 years, and was buried at Flitton, co. Bedford.   He was succeeded by his brother Charles, who survived till 1623, notwithstanding he is at this time stated to be " to the knees in the grave."   The Lady Elizabeth Grey here alluded to was the second daughter and sole heir of Gilbert Earl of Shrewsbury, and wife of Henry Grey de Ruthyn, son and successor of Charles the 8th Earl of Kent, whose protracted life at this time disappointed the ambition with which she looked forward to become Countess of Kent.   Her husband succeeded his father in 1623, and died s.p. 1639.

[c] Sir Moyle Finch, of Eastwell, co. Kent, created a Baronet in 1611, married Elizabeth, only daughter ànd heir of Sir Thomas Heneage, of Copt Hall, Essex.   Lady Finch sur-vived her husband several years, and rejected all her suitors.   In 1623 she was raised to the peerage as Viscountess Maidstone, and five years afterwards was advanced to the dignity of Countess of Winchelsea.   She died in 1633.   Chamberlain says that Sir Moyle Finch left his eldest son but 100l. a year more than he had before, during his mother's life.— (Birch's Court and Times of James I., vol. i. 356.)

the richest widdow in present estate, both in ioynture, moveables, and inheritance of her owne, thatt is in England. The Lord Beawchampe [a] hath a sonne borne, to the great compforte of old Hertford.

February.   In Februarye Sir Thomas Cheeke's wife [b] died. Mr. John Dvn [c] is a Minister, the King's Chaplaine, and a Doctor of Divinitic. Martiall La Chastre [d] in France is dead, and Monsieur de Requelarre [e]

[a] Edward Lord Beauchamp, son of the Earl of Hertford, did not live until 1618, as stated in all the printed books on the subject, and also in the pedigree recorded in the Heralds' College, but died in 1612, as proved by the following entry under that year in the Burial Register of Great Bedwyn, co. Wilts: " On tuesday the one and twentyeth of July an° predicto was heere entombed the body of the right hoble Edward Lord Beauchampe who deceased at Week." The Lord Beauchamp mentioned in the text, therefore, was the grandson of the Earl of Hertford, and the child whose birth is chronicled was Edward, the old Earl's great-grandson. We can quite understand the " great comfort " it must have been to him to witness the birth of an heir in the fourth generation. His hopes, however, were soon blighted, for both this child and his father died before the Earl, who, in 1621, was succeeded in his honours by his grandson Sir William Seymour, in whom the Dukedom of Somerset was restored in 1660.

[b] She was the daughter of Peter Osborne, Esq. and wife of Sir Thomas Cheke, grandson of Sir John Cheke, tutor to King Edward VI. Chamberlain says, " She would needs be let blood for a little heat or itching in the arm, but by mistake the Queen's surgeon pricked her arm too deep, and cut an artery, which fell to rankle, and in a few days grew to a gangrene, whereof she died, and was buried at night with above thirty coaches and much torch-light attending her ;" which, he adds, " is of late come much into fashion, as it would seem to avoid trouble and charge."— Birch, vol. i. 296.

[c] John Donne, the poet. Chamberlain says, " John Donne and one Cheke went out doctors at Cambridge, with much ado, after our coming away, by the King's express mandate; though the Vice-chancellor and some other of the heads called them openly *filios noctis et tenebriones*, that sought thus to come in at the window when there was a fair gate open."—Birch, vol. i. 306.

[d] Claude de Châtre, eldest son of Claude de Châtre, by Anne Robertetz, his wife, was Seigneur and Baron of Maisonfort, Governor of Orleans, and Captain of the Tower of Bourges. Died 14 December, 1614, aged about 78 years.—Anselme.

[e] Antoine Seigneur de Roquelaure, in Armagnac, of Gaudoux, &c. Seneschal, and Governor of Rouergue and Foix. At first he was known as the Seigneur de Longart, and was in great favour with Jeanne d'Albret, Queen of Navarre. She engaged him in the service of her son the King of Navarre, and gave him the share which she had in the Seigneurie of Roquelaure. He was Master of the Wardrobe in 1589, Knight of the Orders in 1595. He was also Lieutenant of Haute Auvergne, and Captain of Fontainebleau, and was created Marshal of France 1615. Died 9 June, 1625.—Anselme, vii. 401' 406.

substituted in his roome. Monsieur de Silerie [a] is gone into Spayne to consummatt the mariage of the King his master,[b] but the event is very doubtfull, the Frenche princes beinge so opposite vnto it. The assemblye of the three Estates is dissolved, and as in our parliment, so in thatt, nothing was concluded, and France is divided into so great factions as troubles is expected.

The Erle of Orkeney,[c] in Scotland, is beheaded, his lands and honnour excheated to the kinge. Sir Arthur Ingram [d] was sworne Coferer of the king's house, but the officers of the houscholld have so stronglie opposed against a stranger, contrarye to the custome of the house, as they have prevayled to have him removed, which must be effected att Michælmas next; in the meane tyme Sir Marmaduke Darrel [e] hathe the board, and executes the office, and shall be coferer.

Marche. Queene Margerett,[f] the last of the Royal familie of Valois, March.

[a] Pierre Brulart, son of Nicolas Brulart, Marquis of Sillery and Chancellor of France, and of Claudia Prudhomme, his wife. He was made Secretary of State on the resignation of Nicolas de Neufville, 4th March, 1606, and Councillor of State 1st January, 1607, taking the oath the 27th Nov. following. He was nominated Ambassador to the Court of Spain in 1612, and died 22 April, 1640, aged 57.—Anselme, vi. 527.

[b] Louis XIII. with Anne of Austria, eldest daughter of Philip III.

[c] Patrick Stuart, 2nd Earl, son of Robert Stuart, natural son of King James V. created Earl of Orkney 1581. Patrick Lord Grey, in 1609, writes to Lord Salisbury, that his brother the Earl of Orkney has been committed, through the malice of his own servants, for informalities in the government of his own state; begs that his oversight may be attributed rather to simplicity than malice.—S.P.O. Dom. Corr. vol. xlvii. p. 14. Patrick, 7th Lord Grey, married the sister of the Earl alluded to in the text.

[d] Sir Arthur Ingram, a wealthy citizen of London, knighted 1612. He purchased the manor of Temple Newsome, co. York, and was sheriff of that county 1619. From him descended Sir Henry Ingram, created in 1661 Baron Ingram of Irvine, and Viscount Irvine, of the county of Ayr.

[e] Sir Marmaduke Darrell, of Fulmere, co. Bucks. He was also Surveyor-General of Victuals for the Navy, in which office he was succeeded by his son Sir Sampson Darrell. —Add. MSS. 14,311. 286.

[f] Margaret of Valois, descended from Philip VI. King of France, to whose grandfather the county of Valois had been given as an apanage in 1285, by Philip the Hardy. Margaret was the last descendant of this great house, which had given kings to France from 1328. She was born in 1552, married Henry of Navarre 1572, who became King of France on the death of her brother Henry III. in 1598. From him she was divorced in 1599.

died in Marche, and she made the Kinge of France her heyre of all the lands which her mother the old queene [a] had purchased for her; most of her moveables she bestowed vppon one of her favorites.

The Ladie Haddington,[b] the Countesse Mongomerye,[c] and the Ladie Rodney,[d] are latelye mothers of yonge borne daughters. The Earl of Tomond [e] is lord president of Mounster, and the Lord Danvers [f] consented therevnto. Sir Robert Drewrie [g] is dead, and

[a] Catherine de' Medici, daughter of Lorenzo Duke of Florence, and Queen of Henry II. She died 1589, aged 70.

[b] The Lady Haddington was Elizabeth, daughter of Robert Ratcliffe, Earl of Sussex, and wife of John Ramsey, Viscount Haddington. He had been instrumental in the escape of James from the Gowrie conspiracy. Great festivities took place at their marriage in 1608. The King himself gave away the bride, and afterwards there was a grand masque and a banquet, in the midst of which the King " drank a carouse in a cup of gold, which he sent to the bride, together with a bason and ewer, two livery pots, and three standing cups, all very fair and massive of silver and gilt, and withall a patent for a pension of 60Ql. a-year to the longest liver of them; with this message, ' that he wished them so much comfort all their lives as he received that day the bridegroom delivered him from the danger of Gowrie.' "—Birch, vol. i. 73. In 1620 the Viscount Haddington was created Baron of Kingston-upon-Thames and Earl of Holderness. He died 1625, s. p.

[c] Susan, daughter of Edward Vere, sixteenth Earl of Oxford, married 4 Jan. 1604-5, to Philip Herbert, created a Knight of the Bath at the coronation of James I., and Earl of Montgomery shortly afterwards. By his first wife, the lady mentioned in the text, he had seven sons and three daughters.

[d] Frances, daughter of Sir Robert Southwell, of Woodrising, Norfolk, one of the Queen's maids of honour, was married on Shrove-sunday 1613-14 to Edward son and heir of Sir John Rodney, of Stoke Giffard, co. Somerset; and he was knighted at the Queen's palace of Somerset House on the 29th of May following. Lady Rodney was one of four ladies of the privy-chamber who, in the procession on the Queen's funeral, had, by " especial partialitie," places assigned them above Baronets' wives.—Nichols's Progresses of James I. ii. 755, iii. 541.

[e] Donough O'Brien, fourth Earl, brought up in England, and much esteemed both by Queen Elizabeth and James I. He paid Lord Danvers a composition of 3,200l. for the office mentioned in the text, greatly to the prejudice of Sir Richard Morison, who had long before bought the reversion of it. Died 1624.

[f] Sir Henry Danvers, created Baron Danvers of Dantsey 1603. He was afterwards Earl of Danby and K G. Died 1643, s. p., aged 71. He was the founder of the physic garden at Oxford.

[g] Sir Robert Drury, of Hawsted, co. Suffolk, fourth in descent from Sir Robert Drury

his three sisters are his heyres; onlye he gave away his land in
Drewry Lane to Sir Henry Drewrye [a] of Buckinghamshire, who was
his next heyre male.   Mr. Edmonds,[b] the clerk of the Councel,
Abbott,[c] a brother to the Lord Archbushoppe of Canterburye, and
Middleton,[d] another London marchant, are now his Majesties
comissioners with the Estates Generall of the Vnited Provinces, to
settle the trade betwene us and them, both for the East Indies and
Greenland; but yett nothing is effected, and I thinke nothinge will
be concluded, for they insist thatt yf they and we shall ioyne in the
East Indie trade, they require that pro ratâ we should beare equall
charge of there garrisons and in there fortifications, and to ioyne
with them in a warre, offensive and defensive, agaynst Spayne in that
Easterne world; which we cannott do without breache of our league
with Spain; and how severe the king is in performinge every article
in the treatie of peace and amitie betwene vs and Spayne you know.
Our desire is thatt we and the Hollanders, as frends and neyghbours,
may freelie, without any opposition on either part, trade in every
place where the other residethe; but the Hollanders do not well

of the same place, ob. 1520.   M.P. for that county 1603-14.   Died 2nd April, 1615,
aged 40.   His three sisters were:—Frances, married first Sir Nicholas Clifford, Knight,
and secondly Sir William Wray, of Glentworth, co. Lincoln, Knight, died s. p.; Elizabeth,
married William Cecill, son and heir of William Earl of Exeter, died 1653, aged 80;
Diana, married Sir Edward Cecill, Viscount Wimbledon.—(Addit. MSS. 19,127.)
Chamberlain, speaking of the latter match in 1616, says that "since the death of her
brother she had become a good marriage, worth 10,000l. or 12,000l."—Birch, i. 444.

   a Sir Henry Drury, of Edgerly, co. Bucks, grandson of Sir Robert Drury of that place,
second son of Sir Robert Drury the elder, of Hawsted, mentioned in the last note.   Sir
Henry, though heir male of the Knight now deceased, was eight degrees removed.

   b Clement Edmondes, son of Sir Thomas Edmondes.   He received a grant of the office
of Clerk of the Council for life 1609, was knighted 1617, and died 1622.

   c Maurice Abbot, son of a weaver at Guildford, an eminent London merchant, and
Governor of the East India Company.   He was the first person knighted by King Charles
I., and was Lord Mayor 1638.   Died 1640.

   d Probably Henry Middleton, to whom in 1604 a commission was granted, in con-
junction with Christopher Colethurst, to be Governor and Lieut.-General in a merchant
voyage to the East Indies.   In 1610 a similar commission was given to him to be General
of the Merchants trading to the East Indies.—S.P.O. Dom. Cor.

tast the proposition without the conditions abovementioned, so as
itt is conceved thatt the negotiation will produce little effect. And
as for Greenland, itt sticks as itt did vntill the East Indie busines
be composed. The yonge Lord Barkelye,[a] your countryeman, is
married to Sir Michael Stanhoppes[b] second daughter and heyre,
the first beinge longe since maried to the Lord Fitzwalter. The
Ladie St. John the widdow,[c] and mother to the Lorde Howard of
Effinghame, is dead, by whose deathe a portion of inheritance is
fallen vppon my Lord of Effingham in the right of his wife,
daughter and heyre to the last Lord St. John.

April.—Shaumburge[d] is now maried to my wife Anne Dudley;
he comes shortlye hether with a purse full of money to purchase
lands in England.

The Frenche, who were planted in an Ilaud in the mouthe of
the river Maraynor, are displanted by the Portugals. There whole
number were 400 Frenchmen, but 100 of them vnserviceable by
reason of sicknes. None were spared, but all of them, allmost to a
man, put to the sword, and the women and children found no
mercye. The Portugal commander thatt tryumphes with this victorie
is the governour of Brasil, who surprised them thatt were over neg-
ligent; his forces consisted of 800 Portugals and 800 Indians. The

[a] George Berkeley succeeded his grandfather as Baron Berkeley in 1613; made Knight
of the Bath at the creation of Charles Prince of Wales. At the time of the marriage
referred to he was thirteen and the lady nine years of age. Died August 1656.

[b] Sir Michael Stanhope, of Sudbury, co. Suffolk, knighted 1603. His daughter Jane
was married to Henry Ratcliffe, called Lord Fitzwalter, son and heir of Robert fifth Earl
of Sussex, in February 1614.

[c] Catherine, daughter of Sir William Dormer, of Elthorpe, and widow of John 2nd
Lord St. John of Bletshoe. She was buried in St. Michael's Chapel, at Westminster.
Anne, their daughter and heir, married William Howard, eldest son of Sir Charles
Howard, 1st Earl of Nottingham, and Baron Effingham, Lord High Admiral of England.
Lord Effingham was summoned to Parliament, and died in the lifetime of his father.
See also page 13.

[d] Count Meinhardt de Schomberg was the principal person about Frederick Elector
Palatine of the Rhine. He accompanied his master to the English Court, where Anne
Dudley, daughter of Edward 9th Baron Dudley, held some office about the person of

French fort, which was well fortified, is rased to the ground.   I pray God thatt Virginia may not drinke of the same cuppe!

The marchants of London, for the discoverye of the Northe-west Passage, have sett forthe a smal barke victualled for 9 monthes, vnder the charge of one Robert Bilot,[a] who bathe bene thrice in Hudson's Sound.   God graunt him good successe!   They have likewise sent there whale fishing flecte to Greenland; and a pinnace commanded by one Fotherbye is directed to finde out the North-east Passage by the Pole.   Of late the Biscaynes have accustomed to fishe att the ward-house.   Our marchants like nott their neyghbours, and therefore have claymed letters from his Majestie to the Kinge of Denmarke[b] to forbid there trade in those seas: whatt effect itt will produce I know nott.   Sir Henry Wotton[c] is nott yett retourned from his negocia-tion in the Netherlands.   The deliverie uppe of the Wesel is nott yett performed; Spinola[d] daylie fortifies itt, encreases his garrisons there,

Queen Anne. Here she became intimately associated with the Lord Carew; hence, as a term of endearment, he calls her his wife.   She attended the Electress to Germany as Chief Lady of Honour, and the court gossips said that she accepted this office because she was not insensible to the attentions of Count de Schomberg.   Her friends, however, for some time, opposed their union.   Mr. Lorking, writing on the 18th June, 1614, says, "the news from Heidelberg is that Mrs. Anne Dudley is now made sure to M. Schomberg." —Birch, vol. i. p. 325. They were married, as stated in the text, and King James was not a little jealous of their combined influence over his daughter.   Anne, however, died in her first confinement (p. 21), watched over and lamented by her kind-hearted mistress, who took charge of her infant son, Frederick, who accompanied the Prince of Orange to England, and was created Baron Tayes, Earl of Brentford, Marquis of Harwich, and Duke of Schomberg.   He also held the office of Master of the Ordnance, but was killed at the battle of the Boyne.   The titles became extinct in 1713.

[a] Robert Bylot probably accompanied Henry Hudson's expedition in 1610, when the latter discovered the Bay which is called after his name ; or that of Sir Thomas Button, in 1612.   In the latter year Bylot himself discovered Fox Channel, between Cumberland Island and Southampton Island; and he, with Baffin, in 1614, penetrated through Davis's Straits to the most northern extremity, called Sir Thomas Smith's Sound (78° n. lat.)

[b] Christian IV. brother-in-law of King James.

[c] He was not recalled until 3 August (S.P.O.), having been absent about four months.

[d] Ambrose Marquis of Spinola, the distinguished Spanish General, born at Genoa 1569.   Died about 1630.

and stores itt with victualls and munition. On the other side, the
Estates are as vnwillinge to quitt Gulicke; so as by all coniecture the
warre will breake out; but the ambassadors here of Spayne and the
Archdukes do constantlye affirm that Wesel shall be rendered. The
townes of Goche, Cleve, Emericke, and Rayz, all which you know
were this last sommer taken in by his Excellencye, had beene like to
have been betrayed by some of the inhabitants in every of those
townes, but one of the confederates discovered the practize. The
cheefe conspirators, to the number of 17, are taken, the treason confessed; the traytors somme are in prison and others executed: the
Marques Spinola was acquainted with the conspiracie, and his men
were in a readines to enter the townes.

In Italye the warre of Savoy continewes. The Kinge of Spayne [a]
hathe in list of horse and foote in Millan above 50,000, besides
promised aydes, fromm the Duke of Florence [b] 6,000, the Duke of
Urbin [c] 2,000, the Duke of Parma [d] 2,000, out of the Pope's Duchie
of Farara 2,000, and from the State of Lucca 2,000. How the Duke
of Savoy [e] will be able to support suche a worlde of armed men is
beyond my vnderstandinge, and the rather because itt is geven out
that the Queene Regent of France [f] hathe caused an edict to be
published thatt no Frenchmen shall put themselves into the warre of
Savoy: neverthelesse the Duke of Nemours [g] and Monsieur
d'Edigueres,[h] the Mareschal of France, do purpose to leavie whatt

---

[a] Philip III. succeeded his father at the age of 20, 1598.

[b] Cosmo II. (de' Medici.)

[c] Francesco Maria II. In 1626, being old and without issue male, he gave up his
dominions to be incorporated into the Papal States.

[d] Ranuccio I. (Farnese), 1592—1622.

[e] Charles Emmanuel I., 1580—1630.

[f] Mary de' Medici, the Queen Mother, widow of Henry IV.; died 1643.

[g] Henry of Savoy, Duke of Nemours, born at Paris 1572. He was brought up with his
brother at the Court of the Duke of Savoy. Died 1632.

[h] François de Bonne, Duke of Lesdiguieres, Peer, Constable, and Marshal of France,
Knight of the Orders of the King, Governor of Dauphiny, created Marshal of France
1608. Died 1626, aged 83 years.

forces they may to assist the Duke, and many yonge Frenche gentlemen (as volentiers) entend to put themselves into thatt warre.

The princes of Germanye thatt are of the Religion are iealous that somme troubles are entended against them by the Pope,[a] the Emperor,[b] and the Kinge of Spayne; wherevppon they are firmelye vnited, and have condiscended to ioyne there forces in a common defence, and every of them knowethe whatt burden they must beare.   The Estates of the Netherlands do ioyne with them in the warre, offensive and defensive.   Here in court there is a great opinion of the rising fortune of Mr. Villers[c]; he is a gentleman of good parts; tyme Rising fortune will shew the success.   All our frendes are well, and no other acci- of Villiers. dents have happened which I cann call to mynd since your departure. God prosper your Lordship in your employment no less good then I would wishe vnto my sellfe, and so I rest your Lordship's vnfayned and everlasting frend,

G. CAREW.

In writing much I may erre in somme particular, and in especiall in forrayne affayres, and therefore you must beleeve by discretion; but as neere as I may I will with truthe.

Savoy, 18 of April, 1615.

<table>
<tr><td>Superscription.</td><td>Indorsed.</td></tr>
<tr><td>To the Right Honorable Sir Thomas Roe, Knight, Lord Ambassador for his Majestie with the Great Kinge of Mogor, in the East Indies.</td><td>From my Lord Carew, sent into Indya. Feb. 13, 1615.</td></tr>
</table>

---

[a] Paul V. Camillo Borghese, born 1552, elected 1605, upon the death of Leo XI. Died 1621.

[b] Mathias, son of Maximilian II., succeeded his brother Rodolph 1612.   Died at Venice 1619, aged 62 years.

[c] George Villiers, whose "rising fortune" carried him to a height of eminence in the favour of two successive sovereigns never attained by any other English subject.

LETTER II.[a]

MY GOOD L:—My former lettre vnto you bare date. of the 18th of Aprill, 1615, wherein all that which had passed from your departure vnto that instant was comprised. You may nott expect from me any other than vulgar intelligence, *res gestæ*, and no further I meane nott to treat of; the distance betwene England and Mogor is to muche, and into whose hands these may fall is vncertayne, wherefore so muche as I may not safelie speake in publique, itt were no discretion to committ to paper.

Aprill.—Yonge Walter Ralegh [b] in duel hathe wounded Robert Tirwett, my Lord Threasurer's [c] servant. Raleghe fled into the Low Countries, where he is entertayned by the Prince Maurice. Sir Walter Raleghe hathe the libertie of the Tower. Your old frend Sir William Lower [d] is dead.

Mr. George Villers is knighted by his Majestic, and sworne a gentleman of his bed chamber, and as like to prosper in the way of a favorite as any man that hathe preceded him; and to beginne with all he hathe 1,000 li. a year pention payed him out of the Court of Wardes. The Lord Knowles [e] and the Lord Fenton [f] were made

[a] S.P.O. Dom. Corr. vol. lxxxvi. 16.

[b] Walter Raleigh, son of Sir Walter, who was still, as appears in the next sentence, a prisoner in the Tower. Young Raleigh was killed in the buccaneering attack on St. Thomas in January 1617.

[c] Thomas Howard, Lord Howard de Walden, Earl of Suffolk.

[d] Sir William Lower, son of Thomas Lower, of St. Winnow, co. Cornwall, by Jane, daughter and heir of William Roskimer, of Roskimer, in that county. He was sheriff of Cornwall 1578, and was knighted 1603. He married Penelope, daughter and heir of Sir Thomas Parrott, Knight, and died in Wales. His widow, in 1619, married Sir Robert Naunton.

[e] William Knollys, created Baron Knollys 13 May, 1613. Died 1632, aged 88.

[f] Sir Thomas Erskine, one of the King's Scotish friends, made Captain of the Guard, and granted the stewardship of the Honour of Ampthill for life, and also the manor of Walton, co. York, 1603, created Baron of Dirleton in Scotland 1604, Groom of the Stole 1605, Viscount Fenton 1606, and granted the manors of Flamborough and Holme, co. York, 1616. S.P.O. Dom. Corr.

Knights of the Garter, and they rode to Windsor as well accompanied
with lordes and gentlemen as any which you have seene.

Sir Julius Cæsar,[a] the new Master of the Roles, hathe married the
widdow Hungatt, sister to the yonge Ladie Killygrew,[b] of Han-
worthe.

Black Oliver St. John,[c] who was prisoner in the Tower when you
left England, about a lettre by him written to the Mayor of Marle-
boroùghe, is sentenced in the Starre Chamber to pay vnto his
Majestie 5,000[li], imprisonment during life, and to acknowledge his
fault publiquelye in all the courtes in Westminster.

Oliver St. John
fined and im-
prisoned.

May.—The Ladie Chichester,[d] the onelye sister to the countesse of May.

---

[a] Sir Julius Cæsar, eldest son of Cæsar Dalmatio, a Venetian, and Physician to Queens
Mary and Elizabeth. Born 1557. Was Master of Requests, Judge of the Admiralty,
and Master of St. Katharine's Hospital, in the reign of Queen Elizabeth. On the accession
of James I. he was knighted and made Treasurer of the Exchequer, sworn of the Privy
Council, and created Master of the Rolls, which office he held until his death in 1636.

[b] Anne and Mary, daughters of Sir Henry Wodehouse, of Wareham, co. Norfolk, by
Anne, daughter of Sir Nicholas Bacon. Anne married first Henry Hogan of East Bradenham, co. Norfolk, by whom she had one son, Robert Hogan, who was an infant on the
death of his father in 34th Elizabeth. Henry Hogan left all his lands in jointure to his
wife. She obtained a grant of the wardship of her son, and, seeing that he was weakly
and not likely to attain full age, on June 1st, 1613, he being still a minor and in extremity of
sickness, she prevailed upon him by false representations to execute a conveyance in her
favour, provided a fine of 10*l.* was not paid before the 1st September following. Robert
died three weeks afterwards, but the transaction was concealed from the heirs until after
the day was past on which the fine should have been paid, whereby the cousins and heirs
of the deceased, Dame Anne Day and Thomas Downes, were disinherited. This gave rise
to extensive legal proceedings, and to a petition to Parliament in 1621 for an Act to cancel
the fine as illegal, and to give the heirs possession of the estates.—S.P.O. Dom. Corr.
cxxi. 16-20. After the death of Henry Hogan his widow married William Hungate, of
East Bradenham, co. Norfolk, and subsequently Sir Julius Cæsar, as in the text. Mary
Wodehouse married Sir Robert Killigrew, of Hanworth. She is called the *young* Lady
Killigrew, to distinguish her from the old Lady Killigrew, who married, in December 1616,
Dr. George Downham, Bishop of Derry. She died the following year. Chamberlain
calls her the French Lady Killigrew.—Birch, ii. pp. 41, 43. Another sister of these ladies
married Mr. Hakewill, a lawyer.

[c] See Appendix No. 1.

[d] Frances Lady Chichester, and Lucy Countess of Bedford, were the only daughters

Bedford, is dead, which gave a new wound to her and the olld ladye.

Sir Henry Bromelye [a] is dead.

One of the daughters [b] of the late Earl of Essex, (I meane Essex-le-grande,) is married vnto the sonn and heyre of Sir George Sherlye, Knight and Barronett.

Sir John Brooke [c] bought of Sir Robert Brett,[d] the Lieutenantie of Dovor, and since thatt he hathe sold it agayne to another.

The Parliament of Ireland is prorogued, and a subsidie graunted.

Dudlie Norton [e] is knighted, and sent into Irland, to be the Secretarye of that Realme.

Sir Humphraye May's [f] wife is dead.

of John first Lord Harrington, and sisters and coheirs of John second Lord Harrington. The former married Sir Robert Chichester of Raleigh, co. Devon; the latter Edward third Earl of Bedford. The old lady mentioned was the widow of the first Lord Harrington, who still mourned the loss of her husband, who died in 1613, and of her only son, who died in the following year. The loss of this daughter may well be said to have given her a "new wound."

[a] Sir Henry Bromley, of Holt Castle, co. Worcester.

[b] The Lady Dorothy Devereux. After the death of Sir Henry Shirley, she married William Stafford, of Blatherwyke, co. Northampton, Esq., and died 1636.

[c] In the S.P.O. is an Inventory, dated 14 July, 1615, " of the Brass and Cast Iron Ordnance of Dover Castle, &c. surveyed and delivered over by Sir John Brooks to Sir Thomas Hamon, now Lieutenant of Dover Castle, Deputy Warden of the Cinque Ports."—Vol. lxxxi. 16.

[d] There were two gentlemen of this name, both of Devonshire. One was knighted by the King at Belvoir Castle in 1603, and the other, who was of Pollond, co. Devon, and Winstanton, Somerset, at Whitehall, on the 1st April, 1604.—Nichols's Progresses. It was the latter, we imagine, who was Gentleman Usher in 1607, (S.P.Office Grant Book,) and who was granted the Lieutenantcy of Dover Castle in September 1613. (Ibid. lxxiv. fo. 36.) He died 1620.

[e] Chamberlain, writing on the 16th December, 1614, says, " Dudley Norton had in a sort almost supplanted Sir Richard Cooke, and gotten a grant of both his places in Ireland, upon suggestion that he was grown weak and unserviceable. But Sir Richard says he hath gotten it reversed, yet with this composition, that he is to have a pension of 200*l.* a-year if he part with the secretaryship, but he will not leave his chancellorship of the Exchequer, because it is the only means to come by his pension."—Birch, vol. i. p. 354.

[f] Sir Humphrey May, knighted 1613. He built the large mansion at Rawmere, co. Sussex, and became Master of the Rolls 1629. His wife was the daughter of Henry

The Lord Hay [a] is created a Baron of England; and the next day Sir Robert Dormer [b] was allso created a Baron, for the which he payed 8,000[li] to the Lord Sheffield,[c] besides other driblettes clls where.

John Daccom,[d] the Master of the Requests, is ioyned pattent with Sir Thomas Parry [e] in the Chancellorshippe of the Duchye.

The Ladie St.John,[f] mother to the Ladie of Effingham, is dead; wherebye the Lord of Effingham's estate is muche advanced, for she had all her daughter's lande in her ioynture.

June.—The Ladies Newton and Edmonds, ancient servants to June. Queene Elizabeth, are dead.

Sir   Charles   Cornewallis, [g]   Doctor   Sharpe, [h]   and   Mr.   Hos-

Uvedale, of Wickham, co. Southampton, and sister of Sir William Uvedale, of More Crichill, co. Dorset, appointed Chancellor of the Duchy of Lancaster 1618, and was Treasurer 1618-1622; sworn a Privy Councillor 1629.

[a] James Hay was a private gentleman of small means, but of great ability and many personal recommendations. He was raised to the peerage as Baron Hay of Sawley 1615, and in 1617 sworn of the Privy Council, and created Viscount Doncaster. In 1622 he was raised to the dignity of Earl of Carlisle, and in 1624 elected K. G. He enjoyed the offices of Master of the Great Wardrobe, Gentleman of the Robes, and First Gentleman of the Bedchamber, to Charles I. Died 1636.

[b] Sir Robert Dormer, created Baron Dormer, of Wing, 30th June, 1615.

[c] Edmund Sheffield, 3rd Baron Sheffield, President of the Council of the North 1603, created Earl of Mulgrave 1626. Died 1646.

[d] John Daccombe, Master of Requests 1614, Knighted and made Chancellor of the Duchy of Lancaster 1616. Died 1618.

[e] Sir Thomas Parry, or ap Harry, alias Vaughan, of Hampstead Marshall, co. Berks, Chancellor of the Duchy of Lancaster 1607, Master of the Court of Wards 1607; disgraced and suspended from the Chancellorship, and put out of parliament for trying to bring in Sir Walter Cope and Sir Henry Wallop for Stockbridge, they not having been chosen, 1614. (S.P.O. Dom. Corr.) Died 1616.

[f] See note [c], page 6.

[g] Sir Charles Cornwallis, second son of Sir Thomas Cornwallis, Controller of the Household to Queen Mary, Ambassador to Spain 1604, 1608-10, Treasurer to Prince Henry 1611. In 1617 brought before the Star Chamber to answer for his conduct as Collector of Privy Seals in Norfolk and Suffolk in 1611, in detaining the money five years in his own hands, and not accounting for a portion of what was levied.

[h] Lionel Sharp, D.D., who had been Chaplain to Robert Earl of Essex, and afterwards

kins,ₐ(whome you left prisoners in the Tower,) are enlarged, and will no more burne there fingers with parliament busincs.

Julye.—Sir Henry Nevill,ᵇ who would have þeene Secretarye with a good will, is dead.

The warre of Savoy is ended by the mediation of the Kings of France, England, and the Pope.

A Jesvite is executed at Sedan for intendinge to kill the Duke of Buillon ᶜ with a knyfe, but the treason was detected before itt could be performed.

Sir Marmaduke Darrell is now Cofferer of his Majesties house, and Sir Arthur Ingram, with griefe, displaced.

The Lord Zouche ᵈ is Lord Warden of the Cinque Ports, which is displeasinge to the priests.

The Ladie Gray,ᵉ mother to the Lord Gray of Wilton, is dead, whereby the Earl of Bedford and the Ladye Herbert receve no damadge.

to Prince Henry. He was Rector of Malpas, co. Chester, and Archdeacon of Berks. Died 1630.

ᵃ John Hoskyns, of the Middle Temple, Member of Parliament for the city of Hereford, afterwards made a Serjeant and one of the Judges for Wales. Hoskyns had given offence to the King by his conduct in the House in the Session of 1614. Indeed so violent had been the proceedings, that upon the dissolution pursuivants were in attendance to warn divers members to appear at the Council Table on the following day. Mr. Hoskyns and others on the 8th June were sent to the Tower. A few days afterwards Dr. Sharp first, and Sir Charles Cornwallis afterwards, were also committed—the one for helping to compose Hoskyns' speech, and the other for animating him. Chamberlain says that "Hoskyns was embouched, abetted, and indeed plainly hired with money to do as he did."—Birch, vol. i. 324, 346.

ᵇ Sir Henry Neville, ancestor of the Nevilles of Billingham, co. Berks, Ambassador to France 1599. He published an edition of Chrysostom 1614, at a great cost.

ᶜ Henry de la Tour, Duke of Bouillon, Prince of Sedan, Jametz, and Raucourt, Marshal of France, born 1555. Died 1623.—Anselme.

ᵈ Edward Zouche, 12th Baron Zouche. Upon his death in 1625 the Barony fell into abeyance between his two daughters, and so continued until the abeyance was terminated in 1815 by his Majesty Geo. III. in favour of Sir Cecil Bisshopp, the descendant of the eldest coheir of one moiety. Chamberlain says that Lord Zouche did not seek the office mentioned in the text.—Birch, vol. i. p. 368.

ᵉ Jane Sybilla, daughter of Sir Richard Morison, of Cashiobury, co. Herts, Knight, and widow of Arthur 14th Baron Grey de Wilton. She had been previously the wife of

Baronet Portman,[a] of Sommersetshire, hathe maried the Earl of Darbye's eldest daughter.

August.—The Ladie Chandos [b] hathe made her Lorde the father August. of a fayre daughter.

Peachampe,[c] the Minister of Sommersetshire, thatt was in prison Peacham sentenced. before your departure for writinge of a sermon against the King and the present government, hathe beene arraygned att Taunton, and receved iudgement to be hangd, drawne, and quartered; but the execution is stayed.

The Bishoppe of Winchester,[d] att the intercession of the Erle of Sommerset, is sworne a counsellor.

Sir Brian Obrien,[e] the Erle of Tomond's second sonne, is maried to the Ladie Sanquer.

Edward Lord Russell, eldest son and heir apparent of Francis second Earl of Bedford, and uncle of the then Earl.

[a] Sir Henry Portman, 2d Baronet, married Lady Anne Stanley, daughter of William Stanley, 6th Earl of Derby, and died s.p. 1621.

[b] Anne, daughter and coheir of Ferdinando Earl of Derby, wife of Grey Brydges, 5th Lord Chandos, who, notwithstanding her marriage with a Baron, obtained, in 1623, a special patent of precedency as an Earl's daughter. She had two daughters. The elder, Elizabeth, married the Earl of Castlehaven, and Anne, the younger, a gentleman of the name of Totteson.

[c] Edmund Peacham, Rector of Hinton St. George, co. Somerset. As early as 1603 he was accused of uttering in a sermon seditious and railing words against the King, and more particularly against his Councillors, the Bishops, and Judges. In 1614 he was again in trouble. Upon being asked what he would give to the Benevolence upon the Princess's marriage, he answered that he would say with St. Peter, gold and silver he had none, but that he had he would give, which was his prayers for the King. He was committed to the Tower, and upon his papers being searched a sermon of a seditious and treasonable character was discovered. He died in Taunton gaol in 1614, and Chamberlain says, " he left behind him a most wicked and desperate writing, worse than that he was convicted for."—Birch, vol. i. p. 393.

[d] Thomas Bilson, born 1574, Prebendary of Winchester 1576, Bishop of Worcester 1596, Bishop of Winchester 1597, died 1686. He took a very active part in the divorce of the Earl and Countess of Essex; hence his favour with Somerset.

[e] Sir Barnabas O'Brien, 2d son of Donogh 4th Earl of Thomond. He took his seat in the House of Peers upon the death of his elder brother, as 6th Earl of Thomond, on 19 March, 1639. For his fidelity and services to King Charles I. during the Civil Wars,

September 1615.—The Lords Willoghbye [a] and Norris,[b] meetinge att the Bathe, in communication fell to yll words, and foughte in the churche yard, where swordes beinge drawne on ether side, a man of the Lord Willoghbies was slayne by the Lord Norris. The jurye found itt to be manslaughter, for the which the Lord Norris hathe a pardon

The Ladie Arbella [c] is dead in the Tower, and by night buried in her grandmother's tombe in King Henry 7 Chapple.

The olld Ladie Dorset,[d] widdow to the olld Threasurer Dorset, is dead, which hath geven a great addition to the now Erle of Dorsett's estate.[e]

The Erle of Lincolne is dead,[f] and Sir Arthur Gorges is in possession of his house in Chelsey.

October.—The Kinge beinge at Beaulye,[g] the Erle of Southampton's house, Mr. Secretarye Winwood[i] informed the Kinge thatt by indirect and mallitious meanes, Sir Thomas Overburie was poysoned in the Tower. The Kinge, who is vnpartiallye just in all his wayes, (although the information poynted att the Erle of Somerset,)[k] gave

he was created Marquess of Billing, co. Northampton, but as, in consequence of the troubles of the time, his patent never passed under the great seal, his posterity did not enjoy the dignity. He married Mary widow of James Lord Sanquhar, daughter of Sir George Fermor.

 [a] Robert Lord Willoughby de Eresby.

 [b] Francis Lord Norris, of Bisham.

 [c] Arabella Stuart, daughter of Charles Earl of Lennox, cousin of the King.

 [d] Cicely, daughter of Sir John Baker, of Cissenhurst, co. Kent, married Thomas Sackville, afterwards Baron Buckhurst, and Earl of Dorset; Lord High Treasurer 1603-8.

 [e] Richard Sackville, 3rd Earl.

 [f] Henry Clinton, 2nd Earl, succeeded his father 1585. His only daughter, Elizabeth, was the wife of Sir Arthur Gorges.

 [g] Beaulieu.

 [h] Sir Ralph Winwood, made Secretary of State 1614, died 27th October, 1617.

 [i] Sir Thomas Overbury was descended from an ancient Gloucestershire family. After receiving his education at Queen's Collége, Oxförd, he entered at the Middle Temple. Knighted 1609. He was a man of many and varied accomplishments.

 [k] Robert Carr, Earl of Somerset, made Gentleman of the Bedchamber and Lord

commandment for the enquirie of itt, wherevppon the Lietenant of the
Tower, Sir Gervais Elvishe,[a] was examined, who cast the aspersion of
the fault vppon one Weston, who was his keeper and attended Overburie in his restraynt: he confessed the fact, beinge put to serve the
lieutenant by Sir Thomas Monson,[b] and confessed thatt the Countesse of Somerset[c] was the procurer of itt, who by Mrs. Turner,[d]
(widdow of Doctor Turner, the phisitian,) att sundry tymes brought
and sent vnto him poysons in tartes and gellye, which Overburye
did eat; but those poysons not workinge the effect, a glister was
administered vnto him by an apothecaryes boy, who had 20[li] for his
reward, in the which there was mercurye and equafortis, which
within a few howres dispatched him. He allso accused one James
Franklin to be a dealer in this murder. For this horrible fact Weston
was hanged att Tyburne; att whose death Sir John Hollis,[e] Sir
John Wentworth,[f] Sir John Lidcott,[g] and Mr. Edward Sacke-

Treasurer of Scotland 1611, created Baron of Branspeth and Viscount Rochester, a Privy
Councillor and K.G. 1612, Earl of Somerset 1613, married the Countess of Essex 1613,
made Lord Chamberlain 1613. Died 1645.

[a] Sir Gervais Elwes was of a Lincolnshire family, and a member of Lincoln's Inn. He
was knighted at Theobalds 1603, (Nichols's Progresses, vol. i. p. 112,) and appointed
Lieutenant of the Tower 1611.

[b] Sir Thomas Monson, eldest son of Sir John Monson, of Charleton, co. Kent, and
brother of Sir William the celebrated Admiral. He was knighted 1588, and created a
Baronet 1611, in which year he was Keeper of the Armoury. In 1612 he was Keeper of
Naval and other warlike instruments and ammunition, and in 1618 Steward of the
Duchy of Lancaster. (S.P.O. Dom. Corr.) Died in 1641, at an advanced age.

[c] Frances, 2nd daughter of the Earl of Suffolk, the divorced wife of Robert 3rd Earl
of Essex.

[d] Her father's name was Norton. (Camden's Annals.) She is said to have been
eminently beautiful, and to have been educated with the Countess of Somerset. Her
brother was in the service of the prince.—Birch, vol. i. p. 377.

[e] Sir John Hollis, of Houghton, co. Northampton, was one of the Band of Gentlemen
Pensioners under Queen Elizabeth and King James, and was Controller of the Household
of the Prince of Wales. Created Baron Houghton 1616, and Earl of Clare 1624
Died 1637.

[f] Sir John Wentworth, of Gosfield, co. Essex, knighted 1603, created a Baronet 29th
June, 1611. Died 1631, s. p.

[g] Sir John Lidcott, of Ruscombe, co. Berks, knighted at Hampton Court 1609. He was
Overbury's brother-in-law.

ville,[a] for askinge of questions of Weston in some disorderlye manner, were committed by the Lords of the Counsayle, and Hollis and Went worthe were fined in the Starre Chamber,[b] all the rest were onelye imprisoned. Lomesdon, the pentioner, for deliveringe to the Kinge a. written paper, which in some sort did taske the proceedings of the Judges in the arraygnement of Weston, was likewise fined in the Starre Chamber, and sent prisoner to the Tower, where he remaynes, and so dothe Sir John Hollis in the Fleet; the rest above mentioned are att libertie.

Presentlye after the execution of Weston, the Erle of Somerset was first restrayned in his owne lodinge, and from thence within a few dayes comitted prisoner to the Dean of Westminster: and his ladie att the same tyme restrayned to her chamber, and shortly after sent prisoner to the Whitefriars, where Sir William Smith is her keeper.[c]

November, 1615.—The Duke of Lennox [d] made Lord Steward of the King's house.

The 9th of this monethe Mrs. Turner was condemned as guiltie of Overburies deathe.

The 2. of November Sir Gervais Elvishe was displaced, and Sir

---

[a] Mr. Edward Sackville, 3rd son of Robert 2d Earl of Dorset, and brother of Richard 3rd Earl, whom he succeeded in 1624.

[b] Holles and Wentworth were each fined 1,000*l.* (Camden,) and Lumsden 2,000*l.*

[c] Sir William Smith, of Hill Hall, co. Essex, (nephew of Sir Thomas Smith, Secretary of State in the reign of Edward VI.) knighted 1603. The Countess was confided to his care on the 26th Oct., and was, at first, confined at the Cockpit, but on the following day, for better accommodation and security, was removed to the Lord d'Aubigny's house at Blackfriars. On the 17th Nov. Sir William Smith reported that the Countess threatened her own life; that she, laying her hand on her belly, sayd; "If I were ridd of this burden, it is my death that is looked for, and my death they shall have." (S.P.O. Dom. Corr.) So well did Smith execute his office, that on the 15th May in the next year he was granted the office of Marshal of the King's Bench. (S.P.O. Grant Book.) He died 1620.

[d] Lodovick Stuart, second Duke of Lennox. He was High Chamberlain and Admiral of Scotland, Ambassador to France 1601, created K.G. 1603, Baron Setringham and Earl of Richmond 1613, and Duke of Richmond 1623. He filled the offices of Lord Steward and First Gentleman of the Bedchamber. Died 1624, s. p.

George Moore[a] made Lieutenant of the Tower, and the same day the Erle of Sommersett was sent prisoner to the Tower.

The 14. Mrs Turner was hanged att Tibourne for Overburies deathe.

The 16. Sir Gervais Elvishe was condemned as a principall in the poysoninge of Overburie, who cast many aspertions vppon the Erle, but more pregnantlye vppon the Countesse of Sommerset, and allso vppon the Erle of Northampton,[b] and Sir Thomas Monson, who was then allso prisoner in an alderman's house[c] for the same cause; and vppon the 20 day followinge he was hanged vppon a gibbett on the Tower hyll.

The 27. James Franklin (afore mentioned) was condemned for the poysoninge as aforesayed. He accused bothe the Erle and his ladie, but principallye the Countesse, and he forgott not Sir Thomas Monson.

Sir John Leedes [d] and his wife, who is daughter to Sir Thomas Monson, for unreverent speeches of the Kinge, and specking to muche of this poysoninge busines, were committed, but he was quicklye sett at libertie, but she remayned prisoner somme dayes after him.

Sir Thomas Challoner [e] and the old Ladie Winsor [f] are dead.

---

[a] Sir George Moore, of Catteshall, co. Surrey, in right of which he claimed the office of Usher of the Chamber on the accession of James I. This claim, like many others of a similar nature, was left unexamined. (S.P.O. Dom. Corr. vol. ii. No. 76.) He was Chancellor of the Order of the Garter 1610-28, (Nicolas, Hist. of the Orders of Knight-hood, vol. ii. 440,) and he held jointly with Sir Robert Moore the office of Constable of Farnham Castle. He was also Receiver-General in the Household of the Prince of Wales. He was a man of great abilities, and a frequent speaker in the House of Commons.

[b] Henry Howard, created Baron Howard of Marnhill, and Earl of Northampton, 1604, K.G. A man of very bad character. He died at his mansion at Charing Cross (now Northumberland House), June 15, 1614, s. p., just early enough to avoid an ignominious end.

[c] Sir John Swinnerton's. He was Sheriff of London 1603, at which time he was knighted. Lord Mayor 1612.

[b] Sir John Leeds of Surrey, knighted 7th January, 1611. He was of the Sussex and Cambridge family of Leeds.

[e] Sir Thomas Chaloner, of Gisborough, co. York, and Steeple Claydon, co. Bucks. A man of eminent abilities, who first introduced the manufacture of alum into this country.

[f] Anne, daughter and coheir of Thomas Rivell, of Chippenham, co. Cambridge, esq., widow of Henry fifth Baron Windsor, of Stanwell.

iege of Bruns-
vick.
Brownswike was beseeged by the Duke of Brvnswicke.[a]

The King of Denmarke in person came to ayde his nephew, attended but with a few horse; the breache was made and an assault geven; the assayllants were repulsed with the losse (as is sayed) of more than 3,000 men; yet the siedge continewed vntill Count Henry [b] with troopes from the Netherlands came within some few dayes marche of (,) vppon the heate of whose approache the King and the Duke rose from the siedge.

The 30. Sir Thomas Monson appeared att the barre in Gvilldhall in London, but for some speciall reasons he was not thatt day arraygned, but retourned to the alderman's where he was formerly prisoner.

ecember.
December.—The 4. Thomas Mounson appeared the second tyme att the barre in Gvildhall; his enditement was read; wherevnto when he had pleaded nott gviltie, for some important causes [c] he was no further proceeded withall, but sent prisoner to the Tower.

James Franklin the 9th of December was executed att St. Thomas of Wateringes, for the murder of Overburie.

The 10. the Countess of Sommersett in the Blackefriers, where she is prisoner, was delivered of a daughter.[d]

The 8. the Ladie Willmott, Sir Charles [e] his wife, died.

Coppinger, and one other who attended my Lord of Sommerset in

[a] Christian II., son of William, by Dorothy, daughter of Christian III., King of Denmark, succeeded his brother Ernest 1611, elected K.G. 1624. Died 1626.

[b] Count Henry of Nassau. He accompanied the Elector Palatine to England in 1612, when he fell in love with the daughter of the Earl of Northumberland.—S.P.Office, Dom. Corr. vol. lxxij. 91.

[c] Sir John Throckmorton, on the 20th December, 1615, says, "On Monday last Sir Thomas Monson was committed to the Tower for business of a higher nature than the death of Sir Thomas Overburie. The Lord Chief Justice said that God had discovered a practice for which the whole state was bound to give God thanks, which should be discovered [*i.e.* made public] in due time."—Birch, vol. i. p. 384.

[d] The Lady Anne Carr. She inherited her mother's beauty, and was married, in 1637, to William Lord Russell, who afterwards became the first Duke of Bedford. She died 1684.

[e] Sir Charles Wilmot was a distinguished soldier in Ireland, where he was knighted by the Earl of Essex in August 1599. He was Constable of Castlemain 1600-5, and

the Tower, were removed from him, and committed in other places close prisoners, and two other of his servants were sent to attend him.

The 11. the Lord Howard of Effingham,[a] the Lord Admirall's eldest sonne, died.

The 23. the Erle of Pembroke[b] was made his Majesties Lord Chamberlayne.

Sir Robert Cotton,[c] the 29, (for what cause I know nott,) is comitted close prisoner to an alderman's house, where he yet remaynes.

The 31. we receved news (which is trew) thatt my wife Dudley,[d] maried as you know to Monsieur Shaumburge, died in childbed, but her child lives.

The last, two boyes borne at one birthe by the Countesse of Argile,[e] were by her Majestie, the Prince, and the Erle of Worcester,[f] baptised in Sommerset house.

President of Connaught from 1616 to his death in 1644. In 1620 he was created Viscount Wilmot of Athlone, and Henry, his son and successor, for his zealous and eminent services in the Royal cause during the Civil Wars, was in 1643 created Baron Wilmot in the English Peerage, and in 1652 Earl of Rochester.

[a] William Howard, son and heir apparent of Charles first Earl of Nottingham. He married Anne, daughter and heir of John Lord St.John of Bletsoe, and left an only daughter, who married John, first Earl of Peterborough.

[b] William, third Earl. His mother was "Sydney's sister." Elected K.G. 1603, made Governor of Portsmouth 1609. Chancellor of the University of Oxford 1617. Lord Chamberlain 1615-1625. Died 1630.

[c] Sir Robert Cotton, founder of the Cottonian Library in the British Museum, the collection of which he commenced in 1588. A Commission was issued on the 20th October, 1615, to the Archbishop of Canterbury and others, to seize his person and examine his papers, upon the ground of his having amassed together divers secrets of state, and communicated them to the Spanish Ambassador. (Birch, vol. i. p. 371.) Sir Robert Cotton was knighted 1603, and created a Baronet 1611. Died 1631, aged 60.

[d] See note [d], p. 6.

[e] Wife of Archibald Campbell, seventh Earl of Argyle. According to Douglas he was twice married, first to Anne Douglas, daughter of the Earl of Morton, by whom he had one son, Archibald, who succeeded him, and four daughters; and secondly to Anne, daughter of Sir William Cornwallis, of Brome, by whom he had one son, James, created in 1622 Lord Kintyre, and in 1642 Earl of Irvine. This double birth is not mentioned in Douglas's Peerage of Scotland.

[f] Edward Somerset, fourth Earl, K.G. 1593. He was Master of the Horse 1602-15. Lord Privy Seal 1615-27. Died 1628.

Januarye.—The Erle of Worcester the 2 day of this monethe surrendered his office of Master of the Horse to the King, in lieu whereof he was made Lord Privye Seal, and allso a larger pention was given vuto him,   .

The 3. Sir George Villers was made Master of the Horse, and the same day (as I take itt) Sir Thomas Lake[a] was ioyned principall Secretarye with Sir Ralph Winwood.[b]

It is sayed thatt the Ladie Penelope Spencer,[c] the Erle of Southampton's daughter, is dead.

Sir Roger Dallison[d] hathe surrendered his office of Lieutenant of the Ordenance to Sir Richard Morrison.[e]

A dispatche is gone into Irland for the removinge of the Lord

---

[a] Sir Thomas Lake, of Canons, co. Middlesex, knighted 1603, being then Clerk of the Signet, made Privy Councillor 1614.

[b] Sir Ralph Winwood, born 1565, at Aynhoe, co. Northampton, knighted 1607, and sent Ambassador to Holland. Made Secretary of State 1614, died 1617.

[c] Penelope Spencer, eldest daughter of Henry Wriothesley, Earl of Southampton, and wife of Sir William Spencer, eldest son and successor (1627) of Robert first Lord Spencer of Wormleighton. She did not die at this time, but survived her husband, who expired 1636, thirty-one years, leaving a high character for all female virtues. She was buried at Brington 16th July, 1667, where a monument to her memory yet remains.

[d] Sir Roger Dallison, of Laughton, co. Lincoln, was Sheriff of that county 1601, knighted 1603, made Surveyor of the Ordnance for life 1606, upon the surrender of which office he was made Lieutenant of the Ordnance for life in 1608. Created a Baronet 1611.

[e] Sir Richard Moryson, of Tooley Park, co. Leicester. He first distinguished himself in the wars in the Low Countries, where, at 18 years of age, he was made the Captain of a company, which company he held until his death. He accompanied the Earl of Essex to Ireland, where he served with great credit, and was knighted in August 1599. He became successively Governor of Dundalk, Lecale, Waterford, and the town and county of Wexford. On the death of Sir Henry Brounker, in 1607, he was joined in a commission with the Earl of Thomond to execute the office of Lord President of Munster, which he held until the Lord Danvers was appointed, under whom he served as Vice-President. (Lamb. MSS. 619, 131.) He is said to have paid the Lord Danvers 3,000*l.* for the reversion of this office, (Birch, i. 167), and that he agreed to do so would seem to be confirmed by the MS. above quoted, which is a petition to the King to allow the Lord Danvers to resign in his favour. The Earl of Thomond appears, however, to have been a better bidder, (see note [e], p. 4,) and accordingly obtained the appointment.

Deputie of Irland, [a] and in his roome the Lord Chauncelor and the Lord Chiefe Justice of thatt realme are constituted Lords Justices.[b]

The 13. Sir William Monson [c] was comitted close prisoner to the Tower, but the cause of his comittment is vnknowne.

The 19. att Westminster, the Erle of Sommerset and his wife, were indited for the deathe of Overburye, and the grande jurye found itt to be *billa vera.*

Cottington,[d] the Clarke of the Counsell, is sent into Spayne, and he carries with him a commandment (as is sayed) for the present retourne of Sir John Digbye,[e] his Majesties Ambassador there.

The reversion of the office was however in 1618 granted to Sir Richard; notwithstanding which he seems never to have enjoyed it, for upon the Earl of Thomond's death, in 1624, it was granted to the Earl's son and others in commission. (Liber Munerum Hiberniæ, Part II. p. 184.) Sir Richard Moryson was Cessor of Composition Money for the Province of Munster 1616-25, and in 1616 was granted the office of Lieutenant of the Ordnance for life, and also for the life of Sir William Harrington, (Sir Richard Moryson's will, Clark, 104,) who received the profits for some time after Sir Richard's death. (Ord. MSS.) Sir Richard Moryson married the daughter of Sir Henry Harrington, and died 1625. Will proved 30th December. His eldest son was knighted at Whitehall 8 October, 1627, and his daughter, Letitia, became the wife of Lucius Carey, the great Viscount Falkland. She was a lady whose character, according to Clarendon, bore, in some degree, a parallel to that of her distinguished husband. (Nichols's Hist. of Leic.) Sir Richard Moryson's brother, Fynes Moryson, was the author of the Annals of Ireland, published in Holinshed's Collection.

[a] Sir Arthur Chichester, Lord Belfast.

[b] Thomas Jones, Archbishop of Dublin, Lord Chancellor, and Sir John Denham Lord Chief Justice.

[c] Sir William Monson, of Kinnersley, co. Surrey, the celebrated Admiral. and compiler of the Tracts upon Naval Affairs published in 1703. Died 1642.

[d] Francis Cottington, a younger son of Philip Cottington, of Godmanston, co. Somerset. He was for many years attached to the embassy at the court of Spain, and was well acquainted with Spanish affairs. Knighted and created a Baronet 1623, made Master of Wards and Chancellor and Under Treasurer of the Exchequer 1629, created Baron Cottington, of Hanworth, 1631. He zealously attached himself to the Royal Cause in the following reign, and having attended Charles II. in his exile, died at Valladolid, in 1653, aged 77.

[e] Sir John Digby, third son of Sir George Digby, of Coleshill, co. Warwick. Sir John was knighted 1605, created Baron Digby, of Sherborne, 1618, and Earl of Bristol 1622. Walpole mentions him in his Catalogue of Noble Authors. Died 1652.

The Lord Roste,[a] (the Lord Burghleis sonne,) shall marrye Sir Thomas Lake's daughter, the parents of both sides consentinge vuto itt.

The Kinges Majestie, the Queene, and the Prince, thankes be to God, are in exceedinge good health, which I besceche God they may evermore enioy.

Foreign news. Now that I have passed over the occurrants within the realme, I may nott omitt somme forrayne accidents. This last sommor, (vppon the conclusion of the articles betwene Fraunce and Spayne for interchangeable matches betwene those kingdomes, which were in handlinge before your departure,) the kinge[b] and the queene mother,[c] garded with sufficient forces, went to Burdeaux, where-vuto the Infanta of Spayne[d] was brought, and the daughter of France[e] from thence was sent into Spayne, so as the marriages are as muche consummated as by proxie canne be required. The Prince of Condie,[f] with sundrye of the peers and noblesse of France, are in armes, and the whole boddie of the Religion are ioyned with them, so as they are very stronge in horse and foote; and for the payment of there troopes they are bold with the kinges *entrata*, which in sundrye places of the realme they have and doe take vppe to serve thatt turne. The iniquitie of the murder of Kinge Henry 4, the displacinge of corrupt councillors about the kinge, the inconve-niences which may ensue by the matche with Spayne, and the con-firmation of the former Edicts in the behalfe of the Religion, are the

Civil War in France.

---

[a] William Cecill, Lord Roos, eldest son of William, 2d Earl of Exeter, by Elizabeth, only daughter and heir of Edward Manners, Earl of Rutland. In right of his mother, who died 1591, he acquired the Barony of Roos, and married Anne, daughter of Sir Thomas Lake, as stated in the text. Died 1618, s.p.

[b] Louis XIII.

[c] Maria de' Medici.

[d] Anne, daughter of Philip III.

[e] Elizabeth, eldest daughter of Henry IV.

[f] Henry II., born 1588. At the solicitation of Henry IV. he turned Romanist, but on the death of Louis XIII. he recovered favour at court, and was Minister of State under the Regent. Died 1646.

chiefest poyntes and motiffs of this disturbance in France: yet on
ether side there hath been no great blow given; the last we have
heard of (the truthe whereof is dowbtfull) was received by the Prince
of Condie, and geven by the Duke of Gvise,[a] who is generall of the
Kinges armye; but itt is conceved itt is nott great, for they which
wishe worst vuto the Prince of Condies partie do nott report of
above 500 men slayne, and in thatt number no man of marke. The
principall men thatt are ioyned to the Prince are the Dukes of
Longeville,[b] Mayne,[c] Bovillon,[d] Rohan,[e] Sullye,[f] the Martiall
D'igueres,[g] Mons. Soubize,[h] Le Marquis de la Force,[i] &c.; and it is
thought thatt the Dukes of Ventadore,[k] Vendosme,[l] and Memo-

[a] Charles de Loraine, fourth Duke of Guise, born 1571. Died 1640.

[b] Henry II. of Orleans, born 1595. He was Duke of Longueville and of Estouteville,
Sovereign Prince of Neufchâtel and Wallengin in Switzerland, Count of Dunois, of
Tancarville, and of St. Paul; Peer of France, Knight of the Orders of the King,
Governor of Picardy and then of Normandy. Died 1663.—Anselme.

[c] Antoine du Maine, known by the name of Du Bourg l'Espinasse, second son of
Bertrand du Maine, Baron du Bourg. He was Baron de l'Espinasse and of la Garde de
Bioulx, Viscount of Montirat, Seigneur de Changy, &c. (Marechal de Camp), Major-
General of the Armies, and Governor of Antibes.—Anselme.

[d] See note [c], p. 14.

[e] Henry de Rohan, first Duke of Rohan, Peer of France, born 1579, died 1638.—
Anselme.

[f] Maximilian de Bethune, Duke de Sully, born 1560. In 1603 he was sent Ambassador to England to congratulate James I. on his accession. He was created Marshal of
France 1634, and died 1641.

[g] See note [h], p. 8.

[h] Benjamin de Rohan, Seigneur de Soubize, brother of Henry Duke of Rohan, mentioned above. He embraced the side of the Huguenots; surrendered the town of St. Jean
d'Angely 23 June, 1621, after twenty-one days' siege. In 1625 he brought back to Rochelle
400 men out of 7,700, which he had commanded. Died in England 1640.—Anselme.

[i] Jacques Nompar de Caumont, Duke de la Force, in Perigord, Peer and Marshal of
France, Captain of the King's Body Guard, Governor of Bearn, General of the King's
Armies in Piedmont, Germany, and Flanders. Died 1652, aged 93.—Anselme.

[k] Anne de Lèvis, Duke of Ventadour, Peer of France, Knight of the Orders of the
King, Governor and Seneschal of the haute and bas Limosin, Lieutenant-General of
Languedoc. Died about 1622.—Anselme.

[l] Cæsar, Duke of Vendôme, natural son of Henry IV. by Gabrielle d'Etrees Duchess

rancye,[a] with others will ioyne with them; which way the Duke of
Nevers[b] will enclyne is dowbtfull, and so may be sayed of many
others.

ow Countries.   The matters of the Low Countries remayne just as they were att
your departure, nether side makinge any attempt.

At Rome ii. cardinalls have beene latelye made of princes, a
brother to the Duke of Florence, a sonne to the Duke of Modena,
and the Archbishop of Rhemes,[c] brother to the Duke of Gvise.

 french news.   The Duke of Aumale[d] is dead, who, as itt is sayed, confessed
vnto his confessor the conspiracye of the Kinge of France his
murther, and commanded him to declare the same vnto the Prince
of Condé; itt is thought thatt the Duke of Epernon,[e] the Chancelor
Sylloye,[f] and the Marques of Ancre[g] had there fingers in thatt
practice.   There is now allso a meane person (who was of the con-

---

of Beaufort, born 1594, and legitimated in the following year.   In 1655 he dispersed the
fleet of the Spaniards near Barcelona.   Died 1655, aged 71.—Anselme.

[a] Henry II. third Duke, Marshal of France.   Being dissatisfied with Richelieu, he con-
spired and revolted in Languedoc, of which province he was Governor, in favour of the
Duke of Orleans, for which he was condemned and executed in October 1632.

[b] Charles de Gonzague Cleves, Duke of Nivernois and Rethelois, Peer of France,
Prince of Arche, Governor of Champagne and Brie, afterwards Duke of Mantua and
Montferrat.   Died 1637.—Anselme.

[c] Louis of Lorraine, Cardinal of Guise, Archbishop Duke of Rheims, Peer of France,
He was not consecrated, but did not fail, nevertheless, to enjoy his archbishoprick and the
honours of the peerage.   Died 1621.—Anselme.

[d] Charles de Lorraine, Duke d'Aumale.   He left a daughter Anne, who in 1618
married Henry of Savoy, Duke of Nemours.—Anselme.

[e] Jean Louis de Nogaret de la Valette, Duke of Epernon, Peer and Admiral of France,
born May 1554.   Died 1642.

[f] See note [f], p. 25.

[g] Concino Concini, known by the name of Marshal D'Ancre, was a native of the
County of Penna in Tuscany, and came into France in 1600 with Maria de' Medicis.
Eleanor Dori, called Galiagi, his wife, was the cause of his promotion.   He was Marquis of
Ancre, Governor of Normandy and of the Citadel of Amiens, and was made Marshal of
France in February 1614.   He took a great part in the government during the minority
of Louis XIII.   He was killed on the drawbridge of the Louvre by the intrigues of de
Luines, who made use of the King's name, 24th April 1617.   Moreri, Dict. Historique.

spiracie with Ravillac,[a]) prisoner in the bastill att Paris, who hathe confessed the whole truthe, which as yett is nott divulged.

·In this gazette you may not expect any more than *res gestæ*. I nether canne or have I desire to comment vppon them yf I could. As other occurants arise, your Lordship shall have, as I can, messengers; in the meane tyme and ever I will remayne,

　　　　Your Lordship's most affectionatt trew,

　　　　　　　　　　　　　G. CAREW.

There is nothinge this last sommer performed ether by the Norwest or Northeast for the discoverye of the passage to the East Indies; I pray God thatt this next yere may have better successe. The plantation att Virginia and Bermuda sleepes, frome whence I cane send your Lordship no relation. I thanke you for your lettre frome the Cape of Good Hope, and as you may, I pray you to lett me vnderstand of your proceedinges in that eastern world.

Sir William Vuedale's [b] father is dead.

Savoy, 24 Januarye, 1615.

　　Indorsed,
　　My Lord Carew.

LETTER III.[c]

Since your lordship's departure out of England (besides this,) I have written two letters vuto you, the first dated in April next after your departure, the other in Januarye, the 24th day, 1615. In those you had a iournall of all the occurrants within thatt tyme. Now I beginne vppon a new score. But first I must thank you for your lettre dated from Adsmere,[d] the Kinge of Mogoll's Court, the 17th of Januarye, 1615, which I received the 18th of September

A.D. 1616.
January.

---

[a] He murdered Henry IV. 1610.
[b] Henry Uvedale of Wickham, co. Southampton.
[c] S.P.O. Dom. Corr. vol. xc. 24.
[d] Adjmere.

1616 followinge. In your next lett me intreat you to continew the
course you have begonne, which is to be curious in the description
of that huge monarchy, wherein I agree with you in opinion thatt
all our Cosmographers are very muche mistaken, and also to informe
your selfe (as much as you may) of the historie and disposition of that
people, and withall to lett me know how you proceed in your
negotiation concerninge marchant trade. All novellties of that
countrye will be wellcome vuto me, but especiallye bookes and
coyne; as for loadstones, except they fall into your hands by chaunce,
trouble not yoursellfe with a thought of them. You forgott, as I
conceve by reason of your yll disposition of healthe (for the which
I am extreme sorye) to say any thinge ether of there religion, or how
the Jesuits proceed in the plantation of the Romishe doctrine, for I
suppose you cannot butt finde mightie opposition by them: of these
particulars I pray you to be mindfull and to avoyde trouble do as I do,
which is to beginne your letter (att ydle tymes) two or three monethes
before you make the dispatch, and yff itt be longe turne your servant Robert Jones (for whome I render you many thankes) to
vndergoe thatt burden. Since my last unto your lordship of the
24th January 1616, these which followes hathe happened in these
severall monethes, but the precise day of every one of them I could
nott observe.

January.   *Januarye.*—Sir Francis Barkeley,[a] a gentleman of good estimation
in Ireland, and a councellor there, is dead.

The Count of Candall, sonne and heyre to the Duke of Espernon,
in France, is a professed Protestant, and to assure the world thatt he
was so in his hart, he nott onely receved the comunion publicklie,
but published a booke in print justifyinge the same.

The Duke of Buillon's deathe was practised by the Count Damp-

---

[a] Sir Francis Barkeley, of Askeyton, co. Limerick, knighted by the Earl of Essex
June 3, 1599. He was appointed Constable of Limerick Castle 1597, and, having
married Catherine, the daughter of the Lord Chancellor Loftus, his patent passed the
Great Seal without payment of fee. He held this office up to 1610 and afterwards.
(Liber Munerum Hiberniæ, part ii. 116.)

martin,[a] and should have bene put in execution by one Captayne Crasse, bothe Almanes; but it was discovered, whereby the danger was avoyded: the French Kinge and his mother lay then att Bordeaux, to expect the comminge of the yonge French queene out of Spayne, and the Prince of Condé, with his armye, quartered vppon the countrye nott farre of.

Sir Frances Verney is dead in the gallies at Sicillia; he led a dissolute life, and mett with a miserable end.[b]

Februarye.—The Lord Rosse,[c] the 13 of this moneth, was maried February. to Sir Thomas Lake his daughter.

[a] This is a mistake. The name was not Dampmartin, but Damprierre, as appears from the following extract from a despatch from Sir Thomas Edmondes, the Ambassador at Paris, to Winwood, dated 10 January 1615-16. "It fell out of late that an Almaine Count, called Count Damprierre, was taken by those of the Prince's armie as he returned from Bordeaux, who, at the instance of the Duke of Nevers, was set free without paying anie ransome. The which courtesie he did so ill requite as during the time of his being in the Prince's armie, he practised with one of the Captaines of the Reyters, called Cratz, not only to have debauched the companie under his charge, but also to have enterprised against the person of the Duke of Bouillon; promising him, in the name of the Queen, a reward of a hundred thousand crownes; the which proposition the captaine having imparted to his lieutenant and others of his companie, to the end, as is said, to have drawn them to concurre with him in that action, the lieutenant discovered the practise; wherevppon the captaine has ben putt vnder garde and his companie disposed of to an other." (S.P.O. French Corr.)

[b] Sir Francis Verney, eldest son of Sir Edmund Verney, of Penley, co, Herts, by his second wife Audrey, daughter of William Gardner, of Fulmer, co. Bucks, and widow of Sir Peter Carew the younger. The career of Sir Francis Verney was an extraordinary one. Late in life his father married a third wife, by whom he had a son called Edmund. In 1598 he procured an Act of Parliament to enable him to cut off the entail of his estates and convey a portion to his youngest son. He died in 1600, when Francis sought the repeal of the Act for the settlement of his father's estates, but failed. The rejection of the bill excited him to desperation. He sold all his property, and is said to have proceeded to Algiers, and to have entered into the service of Muley Sidan, one of the sons and claimants of the throne of Muley Hamet, Emperor of Morocco. He afterwards became associated with the pirates, and finally died on 6th September, 1615, in the hospital of St. Mary of Pity in Messina, (not in the gallies, as stated in the text,) whither he had been brought from Tunis in his last illness for Christian advice and comfort.—Verney Papers, Camden Society.

[c] See note [a], p. 24.

A treatie in France for the pacification of the troubles there.

The Duke of Vesdosme [a] ioyned himselfe to the princes' partie agaynst the kinge; the cause of his discontentment is sayed to be for thatt he·saw no likelyhood that his father's death should be questioned, which, with the mariadge with Spayne, was one of the principallest causes thatt moved the princes to take armes.

Marche.—Three of the Lord of Abergavenyes [b] sonnes, all them beinge men, with another gentleman whose name I have forgotten, and two watermen, were all drowned in a wherry not farre from Gravesend.

The Lord Lisle's [c] sonne, Sir Robert Sydney, was secretly maried for more then a twelvemonethe past vnto the Erle of Northumberland's [d] eldest daughter, without there parents' knowledge, and in this monethe it came to light; the Erle and the Vicecount, though offended att the first, beare itt as wise men should do, and there is no doubt of noble dealinge on ether part. Your good frend and myne, Sir Henry Fanshaw,[e] is dead; his yonge sonne succeeds in the office, which is discharged by a deputie.

---

[a] See note [1], p. 25.

[b] Edward Neville, of Latimer, seventh Baron Abergavenny, summoned to Parliament 1604, died 1622. Chamberlain, speaking of this melancholy occurrence, says, " They were lost by their own negligence and wilfulness, by tying the sail to the boat's side in stormy weather."—Birch, vol. i. p. 394.

[c] Sir Robert Sydney Lord Lisle was greatly distinguished for his valour and conduct in the Low Countries, and was appointed Governor of Flushing 1603. Created Baron Sydney 1603, Lord Chamberlain to the Queen 1604, Viscount Lisle 1605, K.G. 1616, Earl of Leicester 1618. His eldest son, Sir Robert Sydney, was born 1595, created Knight of the Bath 1616, succeeded his father as Earl of Leicester 1626, Ambassador to France 1632-41. Died 1677.

[d] Henry Percy, the ninth Earl, called the Wizard Earl, K.G. 1593. He had two daughters : Dorothy mentioned in the text, and Lucy, who married, also without her father's consent, James Hay, Earl of Carlisle. Earl Henry died 1632, aged 68.

[e] Sir Henry Fanshawe, of Ware Park, co. Herts, knighted 1603. He was Remembrancer of the Exchequer, in which office he was succeeded by his son, Thomas Fanshawe, created K.B. at the coronation of Charles I., and Viscount Fanshawe, of Donamore, 1661.

The Ladye Roxboroughes [a] sonne is dead, to the infinite greefe of the parents.

'The olld companye of the Marchant Adventurers is dissolved, and a new companye, who have vndertaken the diynge and dressinge of all the Englishe clothe before itt be transported, is erected.

Dissolution of old company of Merchant Adventurers.

The Ladye Cecill,[b] wife to Sir Edward Cecill, died in the Low Countryes.

Sir Charles Willmott [c] is made Lord President of Connaught in Ireland.

Sir John Digbye, his Majesties Embassador Lidger in Spayne, is retourned.

Sir Walter Raleghe is enlardged out of the Tower, and is to go his iourney to Gviana, but remaynes vnpardoned vntill his retourne; he left his mansion in the Tower the 19 day of this monethe.

The Lord Brian,[d] sonne and heyre to the Erle of Tomond, by his father's resignation, is made Governor of Tomond in Ireland.

Sir Jerrome Bowes [e] is dead.

Sir Dudley Carleton is gone Ambassador into the Low Countries, where he residethe.

[a] Jean, daughter of Patrick third Lord Drummond, second wife of Robert Ker, Lord Roxburgh, created Earl of Roxburgh 1616. This son is not mentioned by Douglas, who gives by this marriage only one son, Henry, who died before his father in 1643. Chamberlain mentions the death of another son of Lord Roxburgh in these words: "The Earl of Roxburgh has lost his only son in France, a gentleman as towardly, by all report, as any of his nation."—Birch, vol. i. p. 460. He will be mentioned also in a subsequent page of this volume.

[b] His first wife Theodosia, daughter of Sir Andrew Noel, of Dalby, co Leicester. She was buried at Utrecht.   [c] See note [e], p. 20.

[d] Henry O'Brien, son of Donough fourth Earl (see note [e], p. 4.) He was summoned to Parliament in 1613, in his father's lifetime, by the title of Baron Ibraken, and was appointed Governor of Clare and Thomond, as stated in the text. In 1633 he was made a Privy Councillor to Charles I. Died 1639.

[e] Sir Jerome Bowes, of Elford, co. Stafford. He held a patent for importing Venice glass, which he bequeathed to his nephews, John, son of his brother Sir Edward Bowes, and Sir Perceval Hart, son of his sister Elizabeth, who married Sir George Hart, of Lillingston Darrell, co. Kent. He was of the family of Bowes of Streatlam Castle, co. Durham.—Will, Cope 38.

Sir Henry Wotton [a] is gone to Venice to be the Lidger Ambassader with thatt state.

The 27. of this monethe the Countesse of Sommersett, about the deathe of Overburye, was comitted prisoner to the Tower.

Aprill.—Sir John Digbye was sworne Vice-Chamberlayne to his Majestic, and a Counceller.

The Lord Chichester,[b] late Deputie of Ireland, came into England about especiall causes concerninge thatt kingdome.

Sir Oliver St. John[c] was appoynted to be Lord Deputie of thatt realme.

Sir John Gryme,[d] a gentleman (as you knowe) of the Kinges Privye Chamber, dead.

The Erle of Rutland[e] and Sir George Villiers elected Knights of the Garter.

The Lord Rosse appoynted to go Ambassador Extraordinarye into Spayne.

The Lord Hay appoynted to go Ambassador Extraordinarye into France.[f]

Agreement between his Majestie and the Estates Generall, for the surrendringe of Flushinge and the Briell into the hands of the

pril.

urrender of
lushing and
rill.

[a] Sir Henry Wotton left on the 18 March, 1616.—Birch, vol. i. p. 394.

[b] Sir Arthur Chichester, second son of Sir John Chichester, of Ralegh, co. Devon. Privy Councillor and Lord Deputy of Ireland 1604. Created Baron Chichester of Belford 1612. Upon his retirement from the office of Lord Deputy, he was appointed Lord High Treasurer. In 1622 he was sent Ambassador to the Palatinate. Died about 1624, s.p.

[c] Sir Oliver St.John, second son of Nicholas St.John, of Lydiard Tregoze, co. Wilts, created Viscount Grandison of the kingdom of Ireland, and Baron Tregoze in that of England 1626. Died 1629, s.p.

[d] He appears to have been a native of Scotland. Chamberlain states that he was a great friend and favourite of Sir George Villiers and a known courtier, and that he " was solemnly buried in the night at Westminster, with better than 200 torches, the Duke of Lennox, the Lord Fenton, the Lord of Rothsay, and all the grand Scotish men accompanying him."—Birch, vol. i. p. 399.

[e] Francis, who died 1632.

[f] It appears from Chamberlain that the Lords Roos and Hay vied with each other in the magnificence of their preparations for these embassies.

States, for the which they are to pay downe 200 and odd thousand pounds.

Taverner taken and imprisoned, for the killinge of Bird, and in this monethe condemned to dye for thatt fact, butt his execution was stayed.

All the Lord Gray of Willton [a] his lands, which fell to the crowne by the Lord Grayes atteynder, is geven to Sir George Villiers.[a]

This moneth there was in France a generall peace concluded betweene the Prince of Condé and his adherents and the Frenche Kinge, and a great hope of the longe continuance of quietnesse.

May.—The Erle of Shrewsburie [b] died the 8. of this monethe; his executors are Mr. Secretarye Winwood and yonge Sir William Candishe, sonne and heyre vuto Sir Charles Candishe.[c]

Mr. Edward Talbot is Erle of Shrewsbury, but he had not any land lefte vuto him by his brother: many tennants retourne daylie vuto him, whereby he is in possession of somme mannours, and itt is like thatt greatt sute in law will be betweene the Countesse Dowgere and him.

The Lady Mansell, one of the daughters vnto the Lord Lisle,[d] is dead.

The 24. of this monethe the Countesse of Sommersett was arraygned

[a] Thomas Grey, sixteenth and last Baron Grey of Wilton, attainted 1604 with Cobham, Raleigh, and others. His life was spared, but he languished and died in confinement in the Tower, in 1614. Chamberlain says that " upon the elevation of Sir George Villiers to the Garter it was doubted that he had not sufficient livelihood to maintain the dignity of the place according to the express articles of the order, but to take away that scruple the King hath bestowed upon him the Lord Grey's lands and means."—Birch, vol. i. p. 400.

[b] Gilbert Talbot, seventh Earl of Shrewsbury of his name, Baron of Talbot, Furnival, and Strange, K.G. 1592. He married Mary, daughter of Sir William Cavendish, of Chatsworth co. Derby, but he left no surviving issue male. The Baronies fell into abeyance between his three daughters and coheirs, but the earldom devolved upon his brother and heir, who died 1618, s.p.

[c] See Birch, i. 405.

[d] Catherine, second daughter of Robert Sidney Lord Lisle and Earl of Leicester, and wife of Sir Lewis Mansel. She died at Baynard's Castle on the 8th May, and was buried at Penshurst on the 13th May, 1616.—Sydney Papers, vol. i. p. 120.

CAMD. SOC.   F

before the peeres in Westminster Hall, condemned, and sentenced
to dye

The 24. the Erle of Somersett was likewise arraygned, condemned, and sentenced to dye.

The profitable office which the Erle of Somersett had of Custos
Brevium, in reversion of Sir John Roper,[a] is geven to Sir George
Villiers; and the keeping of Whitehall vuto the Erle of Mon-
gomerye.

Sir Thomas Parry, Chanceler of the Duchye, dead.

John Dackham, Master of the Requests, and now Sir John Dackham, is his successor.

The widdow Countesse of Cumberland [b] died att her house in the
Northe.

The 26. the Lord Lisle was elected Knight of the Garter.

Sir William Slingesbye [c] is married vuto the daughter of one Sir
Stephen Broad, in Sussex;[d] she is a very hansome yonge woman, and
he is exceedinge uxorious, and I think a happie man in makinge so
good a choyse.

The Erle of Salisburie [e] is the father of a sonne and heyre.

Brill was delivered into the States hands vppon the last day of
this moneth by Sir Horace Vere.[f]

[a] Sir John Roper of Eltham, co. Kent, knighted 1603, created Baron Teynham 1616.
Died 1618, aged 81.

[b] Margaret, youngest daughter of Francis Earl of Bedford, and widow of George
Clifford, seventeenth Baron Clifford, and third Earl of Cumberland. He died 1605,
leaving an only daughter, Anne, sole heir to the Baronies of Clifford, Westmerland, and
Vescy, who became Countess of Dorset and Pembroke.

[c] Younger brother of Sir Henry Slingsby of Scriven, co. York. He was himself
knighted 1603, and was Carver to Queen Anne.

[d] Of Board's Hill, co. Sussex.

[e] William Cecill, second Earl, K.G. 1623, married Catherine, daughter of Thomas
Howard Earl of Suffolk, by whom he had, in addition to the son mentioned in the text,
who was called James after his royal godfather, and died young, seven other sons and five
daughters. The Earl died 1668.

[f] Sir Horace Vere, third son of John fifteenth Earl of Oxford, created Baron Vere of
Tilbury 1625. Master of the Ordnance 1629-35 upon the death of Lord Carew. Died
1635, leaving five daughters coheirs.

Sir Horace Vere in lieu of his government hathe 1,000ˡⁱ per annum in pention frome his Majestie, and after my deathe the mastershippe of the ordnance. The Lord Lisle hath 1,200ˡⁱ pound pention, and the Order of the Garter. Sir Edward Conwey [a] 500*l.* per annum, and every capten and officer was provided for. Sir Robert Sidney, son to Vicecount Lisle, hathe a regiment in the Low Countries with the Estates Generall in the agreement before Flushing was surrendered.

June.—Flushinge was rendered the first day of this moneth by the Lord Lisle. ^{June.}

The Countesse of Nottingham [b] hathe made the old Lord Admiral once agayne a father of a daughter.

The 9. Sir Frances Bacon, the Kinges Attournye Generall, was att Greenewich sworne a Privye Councellor, and still Attournye.

The 9. day of this moneth, Capten Manwayringe, the sea capten was pardoned vnder the great seale of England.

Sir Robert Cotton was enlardged and sett att libertie: he was never brought to any triall yett; ad maiorem cavtionem, he procured his pardon.

Doctor Billson, [c] Bishoppe of Winchester, is dead, and Montacute, Bishoppe of Bathe and Welles, [d] is his successor, and Doctor Laake, [e] brother to Sir Thomas Laake, the Kings' secretarye, is the Bishoppe elect of Bathe and Welles.

[a] Sir Edward Conway was knighted by the Earl of Essex at Cadiz 1596. He was Lieut-Governor of the Brill; Ambassador to Prague 1623-25; Captain of the Isle of Wight 1624; Baron Conway 1625; President of the Council and Viscount Kilultagh, co. Antrim, 1626; Viscount Conway in the English peerage 1627. Died 1630.

[b] Margaret, daughter of James Stewart, Earl of Murray, second wife of Charles Howard, first Earl of Nottingham. After the death of the Earl in 1624, she married, secondly, Sir William Manson, and after his decease the Viscount Castlemaine in Ireland.

[c] See note [d], p. 15.

[d] James Montague, fifth son of Sir Edward Montague, of Boughton, co. Northampton. He was Master of Sidney Sussex College, Cambridge, 1598, Dean of Winchester 1604, Bishop of Bath and Wells 1608. Died 1618.

[e] Dr. Arthur Lake, Warden of New College, Oxford, elected Bishop of Bath and Wells 1616. Died 1626.

The Kinge at Hattfield baptised the Erle of Salisburyes[a] sonne the 15th.

The 18. Andrew Ramsie, one of the Lord Haddington's brothers, was slayne in the night by the watche in Fenchurche Street, by whom he was stayed, and resistinge, this vnhappie accident ensued.

The 20. the Kinges Majestie in person satt in the Starre Chamber, where he made a longe speeche to the admiration of the hearers, speakinge more like an angell then a man, and he promises to frequent thatt place oftener.

Sir Thomas Dale[b] retourned frome Virginia: he hathe brought divers men and women of thatt countrye to be educated here, and one Rollfe, who maried a daughter of Pohetan, (the barbarous prince,) called Pocahuntas,[c] hathe brought his wife withe him into England. The worst of thatt plantation is past, for our men are well victualled by there owne industrie, but yett no proffitt is retourned. In the Bermudas little good is to be expected; they make some tobacco, but of other industrie I know nothinge. Since our plantation there the ratts are so multiplied, whereof that island was free, as thatt they destroyed whatsoever is planted.

The Ambassader Lidger of Venice[d] (nott him whome you lefte,) is dead.

[a] See note e, p. 34.

[b] Sir Thomas Dale, of Surrey, knighted 1606, sent out as Marshal of the Colony of Virginia 1611.

[c] The first settlement of Virginia was made as early as 1585, but it was more than once nearly extinguished between that date and 1611, when Sir Thomas Gates was appointed Governor, from which time it steadily advanced in prosperity. This was greatly promoted by the marriage of a young Englishman called John Rolfe with Pocahuntas, daughter of Powhatan, the principal chief of the country, which led to a comfirmed peace with her father, and through his influence with the other Indian tribes. Rolfe brought his wife to England with ten or twelve other natives, as stated in the text, where she was very favourably received, and presented to the King. Chamberlain says, "On 18 January, 1617, the Virginian woman Pocahuntas, with her father counseller, have been with the King, and graciously used, and both she and her assistant well placed at the masque. She is on her return, but sore against her will."—Birch, vol. i. p. 388. She never however left this country, but died at Gravesend in March 1618.—Birch, vol. ii. p. 3.

[d] Seignior George Barbarico. Died 27 May, 1615.

The 30. Sir Edward Cooke,[a] the Lord Chiefe Justice, was sequestered frome the councell-board and his circuit; the causes I do nott so perfectlye know as thatt I dare relate, for feare of mistakinge, nether amme I willinge to serche into the arcana of state.   John Villers, elder brother to Sir George Villiers, (by the same father and mother,) was on the 27. day knighted, and placed with the prince, a gentleman of his bedchamber.

In this monethe the Erle of Rutland, the Vicecount Lisle, and Sir George Villiers were installed Knights of the Order at Windesor, whereatt the Kinge was present.

Sir Thomas Ridgway [b] is discharged of his office of vice-treasorer and treasorer of warres in Irland, and Sir Arthur Savadge [c] is vice-treasorer, and Sir Henry Dockwray [d] treasorer att warres.

Barkeley,[e] a Frenchman borne, and the sonne of a Scot, who attended the Kinge here in England, and muche graced by his Majestie, beinge as you know reported a fine fellow, bathe loste his Majesties service, and is now in Rome, muche favoured by the Pope, and bathe, as is supposed, written a scandalous booke against his Majestie: none but one who frequented his table, and had often accesse vnto him, could have written suche particularities as thatt wicked booke is stuffed withall.

[a] Sir Edward Coke.

[b] Sir Thomas Ridgeway, of Tormohun, co. Devon, knighted 1600, Treasurer of Ireland 1608, created Baronet 1611, Baron Gallen-Ridgeway 1616, and Earl of Londonderry in Ireland 1622.—Titles Ext. 1713.

[c] Sir Arthur Savadge, of Rheban, co. Kildare, Knight, Governor of Connaught, (Cox, i. 428,) Vice-Treasurer and Receiver-General of Ireland 1616.   Died before 1625.

[d] Sir Henry Docwra, Knight. He placed a garrison at Loughfoile in 1600, and was Governor there in 1601, in which year he took Newtown.   In 1602 he besieged Enislaghlin and brought the garrison prisoners to Newry.   In 1604 he was appointed Constable of Loughfoile for life.   Created Baron Docwra, of Culmere, co. Derry, May 15, 1621.

[e] John Barclay, son of William Barclay, a native of Aberdeen. He was born at Pont-a-Mousson 1582. He was a scholar and a man of considerable ability, and published several controversial works. He was employed by King James in revising his works, for which he received a pension of 150l. a-year, which, in January 1610, was increased to 200l. a-year.—Dom. Corr. vol. lii. 4.   Barclay died at Rome 1621. He was not the author of the scandalous book referred to, as we shall see hereafter.

Julye.—The 9. of this monethe, att Whitehall, Sir John Hollis and Sir John Roper of Kent were created Barons, the one of Houghton and the other of Tennham, but both of them *en payant.*

The 12. the Lord Hay tooke his iorney towards France; a more sumptious ambassage for braverie and charge hath not beene seene; of men of note thatt went with him, there was Sir Henry Riche,[a] Sir Gilbert Houghton,[b] Sir Thomas Germin,[c] Sir David Murrey,[d] Sir George Goringe,[e] who is now Lieutenant of the Gentlemen Pentioners, Sir Robert Dowglas,[f] Sir Thomas Badger,[g] and others whom I do nott remember; but Sir Thomas Germin in goinge downe a payre of stayres, fallinge vnfortunately, put bothe his leges in the knees out of joynt, whereof itt is found thatt he will never be perfectlye recovered.

The 16. the Erle of Arundell[h] was sworne a councellor to the

---

[a] Third son of Robert first Earl of Warwick; he was knighted 1610, was distinguished for his conduct in the tiltyard, and constituted Captain of the King's Guard 1617. Created Baron Kensington 1622, Earl of Holland 1624, K.G. 1625, Constable of Windsor Castle and General of the Horse 1639. He was remarkable for his zeal and activity in the next reign, for which he was beheaded 9th March, 1649.

Sir Gilbert Houghton, eldest son of Sir Richard Houghton, of Houghton Tower, co. Lancaster, created a Baronet 1611. Sir Gilbert was knighted 1604, succeeded to the Baronetcy 1630, and was greatly distinguished for his loyalty to King Charles I. Died 1647.

[c] Sir Thomas Jermyn, of Rushbrooke, co. Suffolk, knighted 1603, Sheriff of Huntingdon 1607. His son Henry was created Lord Jermyn 1644, and Earl of St.Alban's 1660. Sir Thomas represented the borough of Bury St.Edmund's in Parliament from 1614 to 1640, and was Treasurer of the Household of King Charles I.

[d] Sir David Murray was knighted in 1605. He belonged to the household of Prince Henry.

[e] Sir George Goring, of Hurst Pierrepoint, co. Sussex, knighted 1608. He was a sort of minor favourite with the King. Created Baron Goring 1629, and Earl of Norwich 1645. Died 1662.

[f] Sir Robert Douglas was knighted 1609. In 1610 he was Master of the Horse to Prince Henry.

[g] Sir Thomas Badger was granted the office of Master of the King's Privy Harriers for life 1605.—S.P.O. Dom. Corr. vol. xii. 43.

[h] Thomas Howard, son and heir of Philip Earl of Arundel, was restored in blood and to such honours as his father enjoyed, also to the Earldom of Surrey, and to such baronies

Kinge att Whitehall, and is now one of the commissioners for the earl marshall's office.

The 17. Sir William Monson was sett at libertye out of the Tower, where he had beene prisoner: why he was committed I know nott.

The 20. your servant and frend the Master of the Ordenance was att Whitehall sworne a counceller, who prayes you to pray for him, (as in the Letanye,) thatt it may please God to send him grace, wisdome, and vnderstandinge.

The Countesse of Sommersett hathe a pardon, but she remaynethe in the Tower in Sir Walter Raleghe his lodginge.[a]

The Lord Chichester is retourned into Irland, and for addition of honour the Kinge hathe made him Lord Treasorer of that realme, whereby he hathe precedencye of all the temporall lords, and next vnto the archbishopps. The Erle of Montgomerie [b] is made (by the goodnes of God) the father of a sonne, and as yett the heyre of the erldome of Pembrooke.

The Bishopps of Bangor,[c] Hereford,[d] and Chester,[e] are dead; there places nott yett bestowed, as I thinke.

as his grandfather Thomas Duke of Norfolk lost by attainder 1603. Created K.G. 1611, Earl of Norfolk 1644. Died 1646.

[a] Chamberlain says, " She did passionately deprecate and entreat the lieutenant that she might not be lodged in Sir Thomas Overbury's lodging, so that he was fain to remove himself out of his own chamber for two or three nights till Sir Walter Raleigh's lodging might be furnished and made fit for her."—Birch, vol. i. p. 396.

[b] See note [c], p. 4. Chamberlain, writing on the 3rd September 1616, says, that " the christening of the Earl of Montgomery's young son is deferred, waiting the coming of the King to Endville (Enfield), where the lady lies in."—Birch, vol. i. p. 423. The Earl at this time rented Elsinge Hall, or Enfield House, of the Crown. The infant referred to was the Earl's eldest son. He was called James, after the King, his godfather, but he lived not to attain the honours to which he was heir. He died and was buried at Enfield in 1619.—Nichols's Progresses.

[c] Henry Rowlands, consecrated 1598. Died 16 July, 1616, and was buried in his own cathedral.

[d] Robert Bennet, consecrated 1603. Died 21 Oct. 1617, and was buried in his own cathedral.

[e] George Lloyd, Bishop of Sodor 1599, translated to Chester 1604. Died 1st Aug. 1615, and was buried in his own cathedral.

The 14. Sir Edward Brabazon,[a] and Sir Edward Moore,[b] of Irland, are made Barons of Parliament in thatt realme, the one of Ardie and the other of Mellifonte.

Sir Thomas Ridgeway,[c] the late Threasorer, hathe also his letters pattent for to be a Baron, but they are stayed vntill itt may appeare howe he hathe discharged his accompt for moneyes receved.

August.—Sir Roger Wilbraham,[d] the Master of the Requests, is dead, leavinge onely three daughters and heyres, who shall divide a great estate amonge them, little lesse then 4,000ᵘ. land of inheritance per annum.

Sir Oliver St. John, the 6. of this monethe, is gone out of London towards Irland, to enter into the deputation of thatt kingdome.

The Erle of Tirone,[e] thatt infamous traytor, is dead at Rome.

The old Erle of Exetre [f] is the happie father of a daughter by his countesse, your countriewoman.

The Lord Russell [g] is likewise the father of a sonne, who is like to be Erle of Bedford.

[a] Sir Edward Brabazon, eldest son of Sir William Brabazon, Treasurer and Receiver. General of Ireland (died 1552). In 1571, on attaining full age, Sir Edward Brabazon had special livery of his lands. Created Baron Brabazon, of Ardee 1615, died 1625. His eldest son, in 1627, was created Earl of Meath.

[b] This is a mistake. Sir Edward Moore was at this time dead. His second son, Gerald, who had greatly distinguished himself in the Irish wars, was the person raised to the Peerage. Knighted by the Earl of Essex 1599, appointed President of Munster 1615, created Baron Moore of Mellefont 20 July, 1616, and Viscount Moore of Drogheda 1621. Died 1627.

[c] See note [b], p. 37.

[d] Sir Roger Wilbraham, of Dorfield, co. Chester, was the Keeper of the Records in the Tower, which office he surrendered 1603, in which year he was knighted, being then Master of Requests. Appointed Surveyor of the Court of Wards and Liveries 1607.

[e] Hugh O'Neil.

[f] Thomas Cecill, eldest son of Lord Burghley, elected K.G. and created Earl of Exeter 1605. He married twice, 1st Dorothy, daughter and coheir of John Neville Lord Latimer, by whom he had several children ; and, secondly, Frances, daughter of William Bridges, fourth Lord Chandos, and widow of Sir Thomas Smith, Master of Requests, by whom he had an only daughter, Anne Sophia, whose birth is mentioned in the text; she died 1621. The old Earl died 1622.

[g] Francis Lord Russell, of Thornhaugh, co, Northampton, created Baron Russell 1603.

The Erle of Shrewsburye [a] was buried, with the greatest pompe
and solempnitie thatt ever I heard of any subiect in this kingdome,
att Sheffield in the Northe.

Sir Thomas Sommersett [b] is maried to the Countess of Ormond, [c] in
Irland, by whom he hathe a great estate.

Monsieur Shomberge, husband to my wife Anne Dudlye, [d] is dead.

In this monethe Justice Nicolls, [e] inferior in his learning and integrity to few judges in England, died in his circuit.

Within a few dayes after the Lord Hayes arrival att Paris, Arrest of the
Prince of
Conde.
wherevnto all the princes of France repayred, vppon the 22 of this
monethe, the Prince of Condé was in the Louvre arrested, where he
is kept close prisoner. Vppon his vnexpected committment, the Cardinall of Gvise, [f] the Duke of Gvise, the Prince Janville, [g] the Duke
de Mayne, the Duke Vendosme, the Duke Bvillon, and sundrye
others of the noblesse, fled out of Paris. Att Seyssons they mett,
where they are remayninge to settle there affayres. The common
people of Paris, hearinge of the arrest, in furye they sacked the
Marshall de Ancres house, and made pilladge of his goodes; the like

He married Katharine, daughter and coheir of Giles Bridges, third Lord Chandos, and
succeeded to the title of Earl of Bedford upon the death of his cousin Edward, the third
Earl, 1627. Died 1641. The son whose birth is chronicled in the text was called
William, and lived not only to succeed his father as an Earl, but, in 1672, was elected
K.G., and in 1694 created Marquis of Tavistock and Duke of Bedford. He married
Anne, only daughter and heir of Robert Carr, Earl of Somerset. See note [d], p. 20.
Died 1700.

[a] Gilbert seventh Earl. The ceremonials of the not less stately funerals of his father
and grandfather are printed at length in Hunter's Hallamshire.

[b] Sir Thomas Somerset, third son of Edward fourth Earl of Worcester, Master of the
Horse to the Queen, K.G. 1605. Viscount Somerset of Cashel, co. Tipperary, 1626.

[c] Elizabeth, second wife of Thomas second Earl of Ormond, and daughter of John
second Lord Sheffield.   [d] See note [d], p. 6.

[e] Sir Augustine Nichols, of Ecton, co. Northampton, was knighted and became one of
the Judges of the Common Pleas 1612. He died on the 3rd August as he went the
Northern circuit, and was buried in Kendall church, co. Westmerland.

[f] See note [c], p. 26.

[g] François dè Lorraine, Prince de Joinville, eldest son of the Duke of Guise, born
1612, died unmarried 1639.

CAMD. SOC.   G

was done vppon some houses of his followers, and of another of his owne nott farre frome Paris. The queene mother, beinge desirous to reduce the Duke of Gvise to the Kinges partie, strengtheninge herselfe with the mediation of the Duchesse of Gvise his mother,[a] of his wife,[b] his sister the Princesse of Countye,[c] the Pope's Nvnce and others, sent vnto him to retourne; promisinge him large benefitts; but yett he hath refused to come vnto her, and itt is thought that he will persever in the way he is in.

To satisfye the people thatt there was good cause for the arrest of the Prince of Condé, the Kinge with his mother went to the Court of Parliament, and there the Garde de Seaux [d] made a longe harangue declaring thatt the Prince entended to surprise the Kinge, and to sett the crowne vppon his owne head. The discoverye whereof (as itt is sayed and alleadged by the Queene) was by the Archbishoppe of Bourges,[e] the Princesse Countie, the Dukes of Rohan and Svllye. But the Duke of Svllye in the Court of Parliament bathe cleared himselfe, and the Prince allso, sayinge that he never knew of any yll dessigne in the Prince towards the Kinge. Nevertheless, bothe he and the Duke of Rohan remayne with the Kinge, and so doth the Dukes of Memòrancye, Rayz,[f] and Vzes,[g] with a great boddye of the noblesse.

[a] Katherine of Cleves, widow of Henry de la Lorraine, Duke of Guise, killed at Blois.

[b] Henrietta Catherine, Duchess of Joyeuse, Countess of Bouchage, &c. widow of Henry de Bourbon, Duke of Montpensier, and only daughter of Henry de Joyeuse, Count of Bouchage, Marshal of France. She married the Duke of Guise 1611, and died 1656, aged 71.—Moreri, p. 403.

[c] Louisa Margarite of Lorraine, wife of Francis de Bourbon, Prince of Conty.

[d] William de Vair received the seals in May and delivered them again to the King in November 1616. He was succeeded by Claude de Margot, who held them only until the death of D'Ancre in April 1617, when they were again returned to him, and he retained them until his death in 1621. In 1618 he was made Bishop and Count of Lisieux.

[e] Andrew Fremiot, Abbot of Ferrara, appointed Archbishop of Bourges by Henry IV. in 1602. He resigned his archbishopric in favour of Roland Herbert 1621. Died 1641.

[f] Henry de Gondi, Duke of Retz, born 1590. Died 1659.

[g] Emanuel de Crassol, Duke d'Uyeez, Peer of France. Died 1657.

The Duke of Espernon lyes still and quiett in Bourdeaux, so dothe Monsieur Le Grande in his government in Burgundie: which way they will incline itt is dowbtfull. The Duke of Nevers is sayed to have ioyned with the Princes, but the report is nott certayne. The Duke of Longeville is with the Princes, who a few dayes before the arrest of the Prince of Condé had taken the towne of Peronne in Picardie; whereof the Marshall de Ancre was governour, and in itt a riche spoyle of the money and goodes of the Marshalls.

Monsieur de Crequi [a] is to be made a Duke and Peer of France.

Monsieur de Temines [b] (who arrested the Prince of Condé,) is made a Marshall of France, and Governour of Berry, which was the the Prince of Condé his government. Monsieur de Montignie,[c] one of the gvardes, is also made a Marshall; this gentleman pursued the Duke of Vendosme, who, lodginge neere vnto the Lovre, lept vppe to his horse without bootes, and by the goodnes of his horse he escaped to Lafere in Picardie.

The Captenshippe of Callice and of the Bastill is geven to Temines, and in offices and pentions to the valew (as it is reported) of 600,000 crownes. In lieu of the Captenshippe of Callice, which was promised vnto him, the Queene gave him 90,000 crownes.

The 27. of this monethe Sir George Villiers att Woodstocke was created Baron of Whaddon,[d] (which was the Lord Grayes house,) and Viscount Villiers: he was formerlye Master of the Horse when the Earl of Worcester was made Lord Privie Seale, which, as I

---

[a] Charles Seigneur de Crequi, Prince of Poix, &c., Peer and Marshal of France, Count of Sault, Knight of the Orders of the King, Lieut.-General of the Armies, and Governor of Dauphiny. He fought the famous duel with Philippe Bastard of Savoy, whom he slew.—Anselme.

[b] Pons de Lauzieres de Themines de Curdaillac, Marquis of Themines, Knight of the Orders of the King, Seneschal and Governor of Quercy. He was a distinguished soldier, and rendered important services to Henry III. and Henry IV. in their wars. Died 1627, aged 74.—Anselme.

[c] Francis de la Grange, Seigneur de Montigny and de Sery, Governor of Paris and Metz 1603, made Marshal of France 7th Sept., 1616. Died 1617.—Anselme.

[d] It belonged to the Lord Grey of Wilton, and was lost by his attainder on account of his connexion with the Raleigh and Cobham Plot.

remember, I related vnto you in my last lettre; and about the same
tyme, by the resignation of the Lord Chancelor, he was made Lord
Lieutenant of the countie of Buckingham.

The Erle of Sommersett hathe the libertie of the Tower, which he
vsethe very sparingely; his wife and he lodge together, he lies in
the Bloodie Tower, Sir Walter Ralegh's ancient lodginge, and she in
Sir Walter's new buildings, all doores are open betweene them.

Sir Thomas Monson hathe allso the libertie of the Tower, and
evermore discourses of his innocencye.

The old Sir Henry Poole,[a] (of Gloucestershire,) your countryeman, is dead.

September.—The 21. of this monethe the Ladie Frances Egerton,[b]
to the great reioycinge of the olld Lord Chancelor, hathe brought
forthe a sonne, before which tyme she was the mother of nine
daughters, whereof eight are lyvinge.

The Lord Rosse hathe taken his leave of his Majestie to depart for
Spayne, with no lesse charge and cost then thatt of my Lord Hay,
both of them so farre exceedinge in braverye all precedent Ambassadors as you would wonder att itt.

In Ireland the Lord Awdeley [c] is created Earl of Castellhaven, and
Sir Richard Boyle [d] Baron of Youghall; bothe there titles are in the
province of Munster.

[a] Sir Henry Poole, of Saperton, co. Gloucester, of which county he was Sheriff as early
as the sixteenth of Queen Elizabeth. He was held in great credit and estimation. See
Dom. Corr. vol. xxxij. 172.

[b] The Lady Frances Egerton, second daughter and one of the coheirs of Ferdinando
Earl of Derby, and wife of Sir John Egerton, K.B., only son of the Lord Chancellor,
created 1617 Earl of Bridgewater. The son whose birth is here chronicled died in
infancy.

[c] George Touchet, eleventh Baron Audley, created Earl of Castlehaven 6th May 1616.
Died 1617.

[d] Sir Richard Boyle, created Baron Boyle of Youghal 16th September 1616, Viscount
Dungarvon and Earl of Cork 1620. Known in history as the great Earl of Cork. Died
1643.

The 19. of this monethe the Lord of Roxboroughe is created Earl
of Roxborough in Scotland.[a]

Edward Villiers,[b] second sonne to Sir George Villiers, and brother
to the Vicecount Villiers by the father, was knighted.

Henry Howard, the third sonne to the Earl of Suffolk, is dead.[c]
He hathe no child yf his wyfe be nott with child; his brother Sir
Charles Howard is heyre to the Barony of Clon, which the Erle
of Northampton gave vnto him.

The Prince of Condé was committed to the Bastill in Paris, where Condé committed to the Bastile.
the first night he had homelye entertaynement, havinge no other bed
than a bundell of straw: he is, as it is sayed, to be sent to Bois de
Vincennes, where he is sure to securelye gvarded.

The Duke of Gvise was the mediator for the other Princes: they Reconciliation in France.
are all reconciled to the Kinge, and a declaration of the King's is
published, wherein they are declared to be innocent of any offence.

This weeke, to make this reconcilement the more firm, there is in
proiect three mariages: the first betweene the yonge Count Soyssons [d]
and the Frenche King's youngest sister,[e] yett an infant of five or six
yeres; the second betweene the Duke de Mayne and Madamoyselle de
Vendosme,[f] base daughter to King Henry IV.; the third betweene

a Sir Robert Ker, created Baron Roxburgh 1600. He was appointed Keeper of the
Privy Seal in Scotland 1637, in which office he was confirmed by Parliament in 1641, but
by the same authority deprived in 1649, for his efforts in the cause of the King. Died
1650. See note a, p. 31.

b Half-brother of the favourite, being the second son of Sir George Villiers by his first
wife Audrey, daughter of William Sanders, Esq. Sir Edward was sent Ambassador to
Bohemia 1620, and made President of Munster 1622. Died 1826.

c He acquired considerable property under the will of the Earl of Northampton, and
married a great heiress, Elizabeth, only daughter and heir of William Basset of Blore, co.
Stafford. After his death she gave birth to a daughter, who married Sir John Harpur, of
Swarkston, co. Derby.

d Lewis Count of Soissons, born 1604, and slain in 1641. He never married.—
Anderson.

e Henrietta Maria, who afterwards became the Queen of Charles I.

f Catherine Henrietta, born 1596. This projected marriage did not take effect, for in
1619 she was married to Charles of Lorraine, Duke of Elbœuf. She died 1663. Her

Madamoyselle de Verneville,[a] (another base daughter of the same kinge,) and the Duke of Longveville[b]: how many of these willbe consummated tyme will manifest.

The towne of Chinon and the castell of Bouages in Berry, which places were helld for the Prince of Condé, are rendered vuto the Kinge of France.

The 29. of this monethe the Bishop of Elye [c] att Hampton Court was sworne a Counceller.

In this monethe newes was brought vnto us thatt the Cardinall of Mantva,[d] younger brother to the Duke of Mantva, was secretly married in Rome, whereatt the Pope and the Colledge of Cardinalls were highly offended; he is degraded, of any further proceedinge agaynst him yet we here nothinge.

enewal of ostilities in avoy.

In my last vnto you I wrote that the warre betweene Spayne and Savoy was composed, since which tyme in this sommer itt was renewed.   Don Pedro de Toledo, the new governour of Millan, hathe invaded Piedmont; the Duke of Nemours,[e] a neere kinsman to the Duke of Savoy, and next heyre of Savoy after this Duke and his children, havinge levied forces with the Duke's money, (in his ayde as was pretended,) beinge corrupted by Spayne, hathe turned these forces agaynst the Duke, and annoyes him in Savoy, so as the Duke is greatly distressed, and is in danger to be rvined, and the rather because he

mother was Gabrielis, the first of Henry IV's four mistresses, and wife of Nicholas Damaroal, Lord of Liancour.—Anderson.

[a] This marriage also did not take effect, for the Duke of Longueville in 1617 married Aloisa, daughter of Charles Count of Soissons.—Anderson.

[b] See note [b], p. 25.

[c] Lancelot Andrews, born 1555, Bishop of Chichester and Lord Almoner 1605, Bishop of Ely 1609, of Winchester and Dean of the King's Chapel 1618; which two last preferments he held until his death in 1626.   He was a man of ardent zeal and great piety, and ranked with the best preachers and most complete scholars of the age in which he lived.

[d] Vincentius, born 1594. Cardinal 1615, succeeded his brother Ferdinand as Duke of Mantua 1626. He married Isabel Gonzaga, daughter of Ferdinand Duke of Bozzolo, and died 1627.

[e] See note [e], p. 8.

is not like to have any ayde out of France, the Queene beinge as she
is alltogether Spanishe.

October.—At Yorke House in London, the Kinge in person, ^{October.}
assisted by the Lord Chanceler [a] and the olld ladie the Marchioness
of Northampton,[b] christened Sir John Egerton's [c] little sonne, to the
infinite ioy of the Lord Chanceler.

The 7. the Lord Hay retourned frome his employment in France,
where he was feasted beyond belief. But Sir Thomas Jermin is
lefte in France lame, and feared to be vncurable.

The same day I received a iournall of your days workes, beginninge
the 6. of Marche 1614, and endinge the 27. day of November 1615.
I never heard of itt vntill itt was brought vnto me, which was 20
dayes after I had received your letter, sent vnto me by Sir Thomas
Smithe :[d] itt was faythfullye delivered, and the seales vnbroken, which
I curiouslye observed, because I did nott receve itt with your letter.
I have geven my selfe caution to be very sparinge in acquayntinge
none but your very good freuds with itt, and of them nott many,
concevinge itt to be most agreeable to your will.

In the last monethe the Lord Rosse took his leave of the Kinge,
but he did nott beginne his iourney vntill the 9. of this present
October.

The 9. of this October Sir Thomas Monson was enlarged out of ^{Sir Thomas Monson re-leased.}

Sir Thomas Egerton, created Baron Ellesmere 1603, and Viscount Brackley 1616.

[b] Widow of William Parr, Marquis of Northampton, who died 1571. She was his third
wife, and a Swede. Her name was Helen Suavenburgh.

[c] Sir John Egerton succeeded his father as Baron Ellesmere and Viscount Brackley
1617, and was immediately created Earl of Bridgwater. The child whose baptism is here
noticed died in infancy. See note [b], p. 44.

[d] Sir Thomas Smith, of North Ash, co. Kent, knighted 1603, and sent Ambassador to
Muscovy. For many years he was Governor of the Muscovy and East India Companies.
He was an eminent and opulent merchant, and was often employed by the King on affairs
of state connected with the commerce of the country. In 1619 his house at Deptford was
burnt to the ground, but in the same year the Marquis Tremouille, Ambassador Extraordinary from France, with a train of 120 persons, was lodged in his house in London.

the Tower, havinge beene prisoner there allmost a whole yere about
the deathe of Overburye, whereof he stood indyted, and found gvilltie
by the grand jurye: twise he was att the Barre in Gvilldhall, and
helld upp his hand, but att ether tyme dismissed.

The war in
Savoy.

The 10. the newes frome Italie is thatt Don Pedro de Toledo,
Governor of Millan, hathe fought with the Duke of Savoy, and hathe
geven him a great overthrow: the Duke for his saftye hathe put himselfe into Vercelli, a strong town of his vppon the frontier of the
Duchye of Millan; the particular relation is nott yett come, but daylie
expected.   I pray to God in my hart thatt the brave prince may
nott be vtterlye ruyned by thatt potent kinge!

Manor of Sher-
borne given to
Sir John
Digby.

The goodlye mannour of Shirborne,[a] once Sir Walter Raleghe, then
Prince Henries, and latelye excheated to the Kinge by the Earl of
Sommersett's trespasse, is geven to Sir John Digbye, the Kinges Vice-
chamberlayne.

By later intelligence we heare thatt the overthrow geven to the
Duke of Savoy is nott so great as was bruted, and itt rests dowbtful
whether part reccived most losse.

The queene mother hathe geven vnto the Marshall d' Ancre, in
recompence of his house pulled down in the people's furie, a muche
fayrer house, once Zametts, and, towards the losse of his goodes
pillaged, so many francs as amounts vuto 40,000ᵘ of Englishe
money; he hathe also bought the office of Generall of the Artillerie
of the Marquis Rossye,[b] the Duke of Svllyes sonne, and he hathe
redeemed the Duchie of Alenzon with all the profitts belonginge
vnto itt, which was mortgaged vnto the Duke of Wirtemberge[c] for
great somes of money.

The Duke of Espernon makes a pettie warre vpon the towne of

---

[a] See Appendix No. 2.

[b] Maximilian de Bethune, born 1588. He was made Grand Master of the Artillery in 1618 on the resignation of his father. Died v. p.

[c] John Frederick, patriarch of the lines of Stuttgardt and Neustadt, born 1588. In-vested K.G. 1604. Died 1628.

Rochell, skirmishes hathe passed, and somme on ether syde slayne and taken prisoners.

Sir Henry Gvyldford [a] his house att Toplow, neere vnto Mayden-head, is burnt downe to the ground; itt chaunced in the nyght, and he his wifé, and children, escaped with difficultie burninge in there beds; the loss of plate, money, and moveables is valewed at more then 8,000[li].

Count John of Nassaw [b] is to go to Venice by sea, with 3,000 souldiours, payed by the Estates, to the ayde of the Venetians against Ferdinand of Austria, comonlye called the Duke of Gratz,[c] betwene whome and them there hathe been hostillities for more then a yere past. Capten Vere, the late Erle of Oxford's base sonne, and other Englishe captens and officers, are imbarqued in the service. Hostilities be-tween Austria and Venice.

James Lord Cramborne,[d] the onlye sonne to the Erle of Salisburye, and christened by the Kinge att Hattfild, died in this monethe, to the great griefe of his parents. She is now agayne with child.

Allso in this monethe five men which were planted in Bermuda, fearinge (as they say) to dye with famine, built a boate little bigger then a double wherry, about two tonnes, and, puttinge into itt such provision of victualls as they could gett, committed themselves to the mercy of the vast ocean, and itt pleased God to preserve them, and they are safelye arrived in England. Whatt will be the successe of thatt plantation is muche to be feared; for my particular, I amme hopelesse of any profitt from thence.

[a] He had another seat at Hemstead Hall, co. Kent, where his father entertained Queen Elizabeth on her progress in 1573.

[b] John Lewis, Count of Nassau-Hadamar, born 1590. He turned Roman Catholic, and was by the Emperor Frederick II. made Chamberlain of the empire. He was one of the Privy Council of Frederick III., and was sent Ambassador to the treaty of Westphalia 1648. Died 1653.

[c] Ferdinand of Hapsburg, Archduke of Gratz, son of Charles of Austria, and brother of Maximilian II., born 1578, elected King of Bohemia 1617, of Hungary 1618, succeeded his cousin the Emperor Mathias as Emperor 1619. Died 1637.—Anderson.

[d] Chamberlain says, " The King was his godfather in person, held him at the font all the while he was christening, gave him the reversion of all his father's places and offices, and yet all these favours could not prolong life."—Birch, vol. i. p. 436.

Sir William Dormer, sonne and heyre to the Lord Dormer,[a] is dead. Mr. Henry Candishe, the elder brother to the Lord Candishe. is dead, without lawfull yssue, whereby his inheritance, which is esteemed to be of better valew then 4,000[li] by the yere, is fallen vppon the Lord Candishe.[b]

English ships captured by pirates. Seven Englishe shippes, which this yere fished at Newfoundland, and from thence directinge there course for Italye, were within the streyghts assayled by 30 Turkish men of warre; two of them were sunk in fight, and the other five taken and pilladged, and the men detayned prisoners. Itt is thought thatt Sir Richard Hawkins[c] of Plimouth was in one of them, for he is nott retourned fromme the fishinge vppon the northern Englishe colonye, which Sir John Popham projected, and he intended to make sale of his fishe in Italye.

The Rochellers beyond the Canaries mett with treasure and commodities bound for Spayne, and have brought itt into Rochelle, to the valew of 2 millions of ducatts. The King of Spayne requires restitution; the Rochellers plead the treatie, whereby libertie is granted vnto ether nation to the southward of the tropique to exercise hostillitie, so as nott a ducatt will be restored.

The Mary Anne of London, a shippe of 200 tonnes, loaden with

---

[a] Sir Robert Dormer, created a Baronet 10th June 1615, Baron Dormer of Winge, co. Berks, 30th same month. He died within a month of his son, and was succeeded by his grandson Robert.

[b] Henry Cavendish, eldest son of Sir William Cavendish by his third wife Elizabeth, daughter of John Hardwick, of Hardwick, co. Derby, and widow of Richard Barley, Esq., of the same county, whose large estates she inherited under settlement. Henry Cavendish was of Tutbury Priory, co. Stafford, and M.P. for co. Derby. His younger brother Sir William Cavendish was created Baron Cavendish of Hardwick 1605, and Earl of Devonshire 1618. As stated in the text, he inherited the whole estate, and possessed three of the finest houses in England: Chatsworth, Hardwick, and Oldcotes, all erected by his celebrated mother.

[c] Son of Sir John Hawkins the famous voyager, who accompanied Drake in an expedition to South America in 1595. Sir Richard was no less famous then his father. In 1593 he undertook a voyage to the South Seas, an account of which he published in fol. 1622.

pipe staves out of Irland, within the streyghts neere vnto Malaga, is taken by Turkishe pirates.

Since your goinge from hence (as Capten Manneringe reports) a Turkishe pirat was within the river of Thames as highe vppe as Lighe,[a] which piratt was afterwards taken by Manneringe, and the Cristian captives freed, but of any hurt he did vppon the coast of England I have nott heard.

Thoughe the matters in France seeme to be quieted, yet a bitter storme is feared, and not vnlikelye, for divers of the great men are confederated, and resolved to rvnne one fortune.   Mareschall Dignores,[b] Governour of Daulphine; Mounsieur D'Alencourt, Governour of Lyonnois; and Monsieur Le Grand, Governour of Burgundie, are ioyned in a firme league offensive and defensive.   The Dukes of Nevers, Mayne, Vendosme, and Bovillon have done the like; the Duke of Gvise, Governour of Provence, as itt is reported, is gone to his goverment discontented, for, being in expectation to be Constable of France, fyndes opposition by Mareschall D'Ancre, who affects the same office, and flatters himsellfe with hopes to obtayne itt by the Queenes favour and power.   A few weekes will discover more. *(New troubles anticipated in France.)*

The Countesse Dowgere of Pembroke,[c] who hathe beenc allmost. three yeres at the Spaw and in France for the repayringe of her healthe, is, in this October, retourned with muche amendment of the same.

In this yere 1616 the comentaries of father Mathieo Riccio,[d] a Jesvite, which resided att Paguin (Pekin) in China many years, is *(Geographical notices.)*

<hr>

[a] Leigh, in Essex, about five miles above Southend.

[b] Francois de Bonne, Duke of Lesdiguieres, see note [h], p. 8.

[c] Mary, daughter of Sir Henry Sydney, immortalized by Ben Jonson as

" Sydney's sister, Pembroke's mother."

She died at a very advanced age at her house in Aldersgate Street, London, on 25th September, 1621.

[d] He was a native of Macerata in the Papal States, and was born 1552. He was sent as a missionary to India, and, having finished his studies at Goa, went to China, where, on account of his skill in mathematics, he obtained great favour from the Emperor, and was allowed to build a Christian church at Pekin, where he died 1610.

divulged in print; amonge other thinges he reports of a travell by
land in anno 1603, taken by a frier called Benedictus Joesius, a
Portugois, from Lahor in Mogulles countrie vnto Paguin, from
whence att thatt tyme a caravan departed.   In performinge the travell
two yeres was spent.   And by my curious observation I finde thatt
besides there dayes of rest in sundrye places there dayes of travell was
492.   I conceve thatt a caravan may convenientlye, one day with
another, pace tenne Englishe mile, by which account itt must be above
4000 miles from Lahor to Paguin: yf the extent of land betweene those
places be so lardge, itt followes thatt all our cosmographers are muche
mistaken, and China in the mappes must be stretched farther to the
eastward than itt is described.   The occasion of this frier's travell was
by commandment of his superior, to discover Cataya and to see
Cambalu, which countrye and cittie is likewise mistaken by our
cosmographers, for the frier reports there is no other countries called
Cataya but China, and thatt Paguin is the cittie which our writers
call Cambalu, and that the people of Mogul's countrye know them
by no other names.   There is allso a pamphlett latelye extante of
Corints travell vnto the Mogull's countrie, who reports of his owne
beinge att Lahor, and of your arrivall att Svratt; you have him with
you; of whose peregrination his verball relation will give you satisfaction, otherwise I would have sent you his booke.

Tou shall do well to informe your sellfe whatt those countries are
well over to the northe and north-east of Mogull, and whatt thatt
prince is which we call the Great Cham, for itt is certayne there are
large kingdomes whereof we are neerlye ignorant.

Vppon a more exact review of the booke aforesayed, which makes
the report of the Portugall frier's travell fromme Lahor in Mogull's
countrye to Paguin, which by the Moguls is called Cambalu, I find
by Mercator's Geographie that the caravan took this course ensuinge.

From Lahor itt went to Cabul, seated in the northern latitude in
31 degrees, crossing the River of Indus north and by west.

From Cabul to Cascar in Turchestan, being in 46 degrees north
and by east.

From Cascar to Chialis, in 55 degrees north-east.

From Chialis to Turphan, in 56 degrees north-east.

From Turpham to Camul, in 58 degrees north-east and by east.

From Camul to Sociev, or Savcy, within the Tartars' Wall, in 48 degrees due south.

From Sociev, or Savcy, to Paguin, the chiefe cittie in China, called by the Mogulls Cambalv, southe-east, and four monethes iourney.

Lahor, as I take itt, stands in 23 degrees to the northe of the line, and Pagum or Cambalv in 45 degrees of latitude, which is 22 degrees more to the northe then Lahor, so as itt appears that the next way for the caravan to have gone had been much shorter by a more easterlye course then to descend, as itt did, vnto 58 degrees of northe latitude, which was the cause of the longe travell, otherwise itt is most certayne thatt the voyage might have bene performed in lesse then 492 days.

I suppose that necessitie did enforce them vnto itt, the next way not beinge passable, by reason of mightie rivers, or some other natural impediment of mountaynes and desartes; wherefore I do correct my former opinion, that Asia ought to have a longer extent to the eastward then in the mappes is described, concevinge thatt from Lahor to Paguin in a right lyne, there is nott little more then 2,000 myle Englishe.   Of this curiositie I pray you to enforme your selfe.

This last sommer 25 Portugalls and 3 French friers (which were lefte in Brasil when the Rivardine and the French plantation was defeated,[a]) fittinge themselves with canoes passed vppe the river of Amazons, allmost as highe as to Quito in the northe part of Peru, and fromme thence overland vnto Carthagena: this paynfull iurney they perfourmed in tenne monethes, and from thence they were embarqued for Spayne.   In the Tercera an Englishe mr. saw theme, who reportes by there relations, thatt they saw more gold (as they conceve) then any former tymes hathe discovered: itt is able to sett a man's

[a] See page 6.

hart on fire to make proofe of suche a fortune, but how to effect itt, *hoc opus hic labor est.* The observation I make is that the land of America is not a country of so large an extent as we conceve itt to be, but in breadthe muche lesse then is supposed, otherwise itt was impossible for these Portugalls to have perfourmed there voyadge in so few monethes.

The Northwest passage hathe this last sommer bene attempted, but nothinge effected, and nowe lesse hope to fynd itt then heretofore.

NOVEMBER. *November.*—The newes frome the Low Countries is thatt Count
News from the Henry of Nassav [a] shall marrye the daughter of the Lantzgrave of
Low Countries. Hesse: her portion is sayed to be 100,000 rex dollars. She is to be delivered att Arnham, and maried at the Hage.

From Italie we heare thatt the Duke of Savoy lies betwene two fires; in Piemont he is assayled by the Kinge of Spaynes armie, commanded by Don Pedro de Toledo, Governour of Millan, and in Savoy by the Duke of Nemours, his vnnaturall kinsman. In Piemont he hathe latelye lost a small towne called St. Germain, where the Spaniards fortifie.

Creation of the The 4. of this monethe the prince was created Prince of Wales and
Prince of Wales. Erle of Chester at Whitehall, with such pompe and solempnitie as hathe beene accustomed.

At this great trivmphe the Erle of Arundell was Erle Marshall,[b] and 26 noblemen's sonnes made Knights of the Bathe: *the list of there names* you shall receve with these, and also the *names of the Prince's officers,* as well of *his house as landes.*

Note.—I cannott perfourme this promise, for att closinge vppe of this gazette the prince's house was not settled. In my next letter itt shall nott be omitted.

---

[a] Henry Frederick, son of William Prince of Orange, born Feb. 1584, and succeeded his brother Maurice as Prince of Orange 1625. Died 1647. He married, 1625, Amalia daughter of John Albert Count of Solms.—Anderson, 544.

[b] Thomas Howard, created Earl Marshal at the time of the baptism of the son of Sir John Egerton, see n. [c], p. 47. Died 1646.

The manner of the prince's creation was this:[a] his Majestie beinge set in his chayre vnder the clothe of estate, the Knights of the Bathe presented themselves in there purple robes, making a gvarde throughe the which the prince was to passe; then the Erle Marshall and the Lord Chamberlayne[b] in there robes folowed; next vnto them Garter the principall Kinge at Armes[c] with the letters pattents in his hand; after whome the Erle of Sussex,[d] bearing the purple ermined robe, the trayne whereof was supported by the Erle of Huntingdon;[e] the Erle of Rutland[f] bare the sword with the pomell vppeward, the Erle of Derby[g] the ringe, the Erle of Shrewsbury[h] the golden rodde, the Duke of Lennox the cappe and coronet; then followed the prince in his purple kirtle, supported by the Lord Threasorer[i] and the Lord Admirall.[k] When the prince was come to the Kinge he kneeled, and so remayned kneelinge vntill the letters pattents were read by Mr. Secretarye Winwood, in the readinge whereof his robe and princelye ensignes were delivered and put vppon him; which done, he retourned in the same forme he came into the hall, his trayne beinge borne by the Erle of Huntingdon. At dynner in the hall he sat in his robes, his cappe and coronet on his head, and the lordes aforesayed (which did the services above mentioned) in there robes dyned with him.   The rest of the tryumphe was barriers, playes, and roninge at the ringe, which lasted two dayes.

The 7. of this monethe the Lord Chanceler was created att Whitehall Vicecount Brackley, the Lord Knowlles Vicount Wallingford, and Sir Phillippe Stanhope Lord Stanhope of Shelford.[l]

[a] This ceremonial is described at length in Nichols's Progresses, &c. of James I. vol. iii. p. 212.   [b] The Earl of Pembroke.

[c] William Segar, appointed Somerset Herald 1589, Norroy 1593, Garter 1603, knighted November in this year.   Died 1633.

[d] Robert Ratcliffe, fifth Earl. Died 1629, s. p.   [e] Henry Hastings, fifth Earl. Died 1643.

[f] Francis Manners, sixth Earl. Died 1632.   [g] William Stanley, sixth Earl. Died 1642.

[h] Edward Talbot, eighth Earl.   Died 1618.

[i] Earl of Suffolk.   [k] Lord Howard of Effingham.

[l] Eldest son of Sir John Stanhope of Elvaston, co. Derby, knighted 1605, created

The 12. Sir John Tindall,[a] a man of seventy-two years of age, and one of the Masters of the Chancerie, as he came frome Westminster Hall, was slayne at his chamber dore in Lincoln's Inn by one called Bertram,[b] an aged man of seventy five-yeres, for making of some vniust report (as he alleadgethe) in a cause of his which depended in the Chancerye: the fact is very strange, and especiallie to be committed by a man of his yeres. Att his apprehension (which was instantlye in the place) he sayed he was nott sorrye for his wicked deed. Tindal had killed him with two reports, and in killing of him he deed no more harme then in killinge a theefe or robber vppon the higheway. He is in the King's Bench; what he will say att his arraygnement that day will produce.

The Marques of Ancre, Marshall of France, is latelye created Duke of Ancre and peere of France; and itt is a common brute thatt he shall be made shortly Constable of France.

The 17. Bertrame hanged himselfe in prison, where he hathe prevented the hangman.

The 18. Sir Henry Montagew,[c] the Kinges Sergeant and Recorder of London, was sworne in the Kinges Benche in Westminster Hall Lord Chiefe Justice, in the place of Sir Edward Cooke, who now is dischardged from his chancellershippe,[d] and all other offices in the common wealthe: *sic transit gloria mundi*, wherein he was a powerfull man.

Sir Thomas Jermin is retourned out of France and in some de-

Baron Stanhope of Shelford, co. Notts, 1616, and Earl of Chesterfield 1628. He greatly distinguished himself by his loyalty in the next reign, particularly in the defence of Lichfield in 1642-3, at the capture of which he was taken prisoner, and died in confinement 1656, aged 72.

   [a] Sir John Tindal, D.C.L., of Norfolk, was knighted 1603.

   [b] His wife was sister or half-sister to Sir Robert Chamberlain's father.—Birch, i. 443.

   [c] Grandson of Lord Chief Justice Montagu. He was an eminent lawyer, knighted and elected Recorder of London 1603, made Sergeant-at-Law and King's Sergeant 1610, Lord Chief Justice 1616, Lord High Treasurer of England, Baron Montague, and Viscount Mandeville 1620, Lord President of the Council 1621, Earl of Manchester, 1625, and Lord Keeper 1627. Died 1642.

   [d] *Read* chief-justiceship.

spayre of any hope to recover the use of his leggs, nott yett haveinge
strength sufficient to go with crooches.

Sancerre, in Berry, beinge one of the cavtionarye townes which Foreign news.
those of the religion in France had in there possession for the exercise of religion, hathe latelye bene troubled by the Count de Maran,[a]
sonne and heyre to the Count de Sancerre, a catholique; he bathe
surprised the castle and put a stronge guard of companies into itt,
which annoyes the cittizens very muche; butt itt is thought thatt the
Kinge will take order for the pacifyinge-of the present trouble, and
give the Sancerrers satisfaction.

The towne of Peronne, in Picardie,[b] which in August last was
taken by the Duke of Longveville frome the Duke of Ancre, is, by
the Kinges edict, approved to be well done, and the government of it
confirmed vnto Longueville.

The Duke of Espernon continewes his enterprise agaynst the Rochellers, and bathe taken from them a little towne called Surgeres.
The Kinge hathe sent Monsieur de Boyssisye,[c] an ancient councceller
of estate, to appease the troubles betwene the Duke and the Rochellers,
but nothinge is yett effected.

The warre continewes in Savoy and Piemont. To confront the
governour of Myllan, in Piemont, the Duke hathe an armye commanded by himsellfe in person; in Savoy he hathe another commanded by his eldest sonne (Don Vittorio), to resist the designes of the
Duke de Nemours; and a third in Monferrat, to keepe the possession
of suche places as there do belonge vnto him. Yf God do nott move
the harts of some Christian princes to give him assistance, itt is to be
feared thatt Spayne will devour him, which will be a terror to Italye,
and inconvenient for France.

Not many dayes past, in Paris, the Count de Avvergne [d] made a

<hr>

[a] Rene de Bueil, Count de Maran, son of Jean VII. of that name, Count de Sancerre,
by Anne, daughter of Guy de Daillon Count du Lude. In 1626 he married Frances do
Montalais, and in 1638 succeeded his father as Count of Sancerre.—Moreri.

[b] See page 43.

[c] Jean de Thumery, Seigneur de Boissise, Ambassador to England 1591-1601.

[d] Charles de Valois, natural son of Charles IX., by Mary, daughter of John Touchet,

CAMD. SOC.

feast: to adde magnificence vnto itt, (att supper tyme,) certayne
chambers and small shott were discharged; this gave an alarme to the
Kinge and Queene in the Lovre, and wrought amazement in them,
dowbting of some treason; the townsmen beganne to arme, and
Monsieur de Temines (who hathe the chardge of the Prince of Condé
in the Bastille) feared that some attempt would be given to set the
Prince att libertie, and demanded of the Prince whether he were
privie to any suche intention, for yf suche, (sayed he,) I must do my
dutie. What! (sayed the prince,) would you then kill me? I say
nott so, (replied Temines,) but I must do my dutie. These dowbtfull answeres amazed the . Prince, and nott without cause in my
opinion, but in a moment, (when the truthe was knowne,) feares on
all sides vanished. The next day the Prince's servants which attended
him were removed, whereatt he took such a melanchollye, that untill
extreme hunger pinched him he did not eate, and itt was feared he
would have famished himself.

The 19. I received letters out of Spayne. The West Indies fleet
is daylye expected. There is now in St. Sebastian's 17 great shipps
of 400 tonnes and vpwards in bvilding, and 6 great shipps of
600 tonnes and upward, sent from thence to Sevilla, which are
bought for the Kinges vse. About 3 monethes past an offender
was harbored in the Duke of Alva[a] his house (the Duke nott beinge
att home): the officers entred the house and attached him. The
Duchesse, conceving itt to be a touche to her honnour to have him
taken in her house, commanded her servants to reskew him, which
they did, so as he made an escape. Vppon complaynt made vnto
the Kinge, the Duke approved his wives act; in the end he fell into
the Kinges displeasure, and is sentenced to forbear his repayre to
the court for the terme of five years. The warre in Piemont and
Savoy keepes the Netherlands in peace, for the Kinge is resolved to
breake the truce about the matter of Cleve, but now he is nott at

born 1572. He was first Grand Prior of France, then Count of Auvergne, and afterwards
Duke d'Angoulême.

[a] Antoine Alvarez de Toledo, grandson of Ferdinand, the celebrated Duke of Alva.
He married Mencie de Mendoza, daughter of Iuico, Duke of Infantado, and died 1640.

leasure.   The Duke of Lerma [a] holds his greatnes, yett somewhatt diminished by reason of a destraction betweene him and his sonne the Duke of Vzeda.   Heretofore, he was the referendarye betweene the Kinge and him, and in a manner all things were managed by the Duke of Vzeda; but now his father hathe taken all his papers from him, and the Kinge, seeing that betweene the father and the sonne his busines receved hinderance, beginnes to looke into his affayres himself, which is some abatement of there greatnesse.

There is in Spayne a common report that the Kinge of Spayne shall marry the Duke of Florance's sister; but wise men are of opinion that he will never marrye.

I will now tell you a wonder, the strangenesse of it will hardlye *A watery* induce you to believe itt, but yett (as I do) bestow an historical *planet.* faythe vppon itt.   I had itt of the Lord Threasurer, and as neare as I canne I will faythfully report itt.   There was here in London a marchant called Mr. Havers, who was a great assurer of goodes, (a common trade in the Cittie,) and thereby he was growne into a good estate and esteemed to be worth 30 or 40,000^{li}.   About Michellmas last, sittinge in his comtinge house, he was stroken with a waterye plannet, and, findinge himsellfe to be presentlye mortallye sicke, in his cash or day booke, (writinge downe the day of the monethe,) this day (sayde he) I was stroken with a waterye plannet, Lord have mercye vppon me! which done, goinge towardes his chamber, (his face and brest being all wett,) being demanded how he did, I am (sayed he) stroken with a waterye plannet, Lord have mercye vppon me! and lying nott past three dayes sicke he died.   This, in my opinion, is one of the strangest thinges thatt I ever heard of, he

[a] The Duke of Lerma was the chief favourite of Philip III.   So great was his influence with that monarch, that he got himself, his son the Duke of Uzeda, and his grandson the Duke of Cea all made grandees of Spain.   Philip IV. upon his accession, chiefly through the jealousy and machinations of the Duke of Uzeda, dismissed all the Duke of Lerma's creatures about the Court, and he, apprehending that the storm against his dependants might fall also upon himself, took shelter under a cardinal's hat.   He retired to Valladolid, where he took part in the services of the church, and passed his old age in devotion and exercises of piety.

beinge the first man thatt I ever heard of to dye by ·a waterye planet; and what this moyst plannet meaneth I am meerelye ignorant.

General news. The Lord Dormer is dead in this monethe. The wardshippe of his grandchild and heyre is given to the Erle of Mongomerye. Coventry,[a] who this sommer was a reader in the Middle Temple, is (in the roome of Sir Henry Montagew) Recorder of London. Sir Lionell Cranfield [b] is made one of the Masters of the Requests, and nott longe before (in the place of Sir John Dackum) when he was advanced to be Chanceler of the Duchye, one called Robert Nanton,[c] (now knighted) succeeded him in the Mastershippe of the Requests.

A French gentleman called [d], for speakinge to liberallye to the dishonnour of the Frenche Queene Dowager and the Duke of Ancre, was sentenced to death. First he was hanged, then his head cut of, and, lastlye, burnt to ashes. This execution was in Paris.

The Erle of Sommerset by his Majesties permission (to geve him somme comefort in his imprisonment) was longe since removed to his wives lodginge, where they have agreed so well as she is with child.

You have heard of one Roberts of Truro in Cornwall, an overgrowne ryche man (beinge now dead) his sonne and heyre Richard Roberts (tickled with a desire of honnour), to be knighted hath sent vnto the Kinge 12,000[li], to be repayed vnto him by 1,200[li] yeerly until the debt be payed, so as vppon the matter the interest payes the debt. I would more suche Roberts might be found.[e]

---

[a] Thomas Coventry, son of Thomas Coventry, Judge of the Common Pleas. His appointment to the Recordership gave great offence to the King. He seems, however, soon to have made his way at Court, for in March 1617 he was made Solicitor-General, and knighted, Attorney-General 1620, Lord Keeper 1625, and created Baron Coventry 1628. Died 1640.

[b] Afterwards Lord Treasurer and the celebrated Earl of Middlesex. Disgraced 1624. Died 1645.

[c] Knighted 1615, Secretary of State 1618, and afterwards Master of the Court of Wards. Died 1635.

[d] Blank in the original.

[e] Chamberlain gives a somewhat different account of this affair. Speaking of the King's intended journey to Scotland he says, "But all the difficulty will be for money to bear the

The Turkes, who in former times knew nott any other then the Turkish pirates. Mediterran Sea, nor other shipps of warre then galles, have of late yeres (as you know) begonne to enter into the knowledge of crosse sayles, wherein now they are growne as perfitt as Christians. There belonges at this present the number of 70 shippes (the most whereof are above 200 tonnes) vnto the towne Angire: they do not onlye take and spoyle all Christians thatt trade in the Levant, (which our Englishe marchantes to their great loss have felt,) but the coasts of Spayne and Barbarie (without the Streyghts) receves incredible damage by them, and of late eighteen of these Turkishe pirattes sayled to the Azores, and landed in the Isle of St. Marie and spoyled all the iland, takinge all the inhabitants, men, women, and children, prisoners, leavinge the same desolate. Itt is feared thatt this next sommer they will seeke for purchase vppon the coasts of England and Irland. In the towne of Angire (as heretofore) the Englishe are well enoughe intreated, but yf they be taken at sea, ether outward or homeward bound, they are esteemed good price without redemption. Yf the Christian princes do nott by an vnanyme (*sic*) consent endeavour there suppression, there coastes will be daylye infested, and the trade into the Levant will be vtterlye destroyed, for the numbers of pirattes encrease like Hidraes, and there shipps are for the most part manned with voluntarye renegados of all nations; but, to assure themselves of these renegados, the Turkes are so carefull as in every shippe there is three Turkes for one renegado.

journey, which how to compass all projects must be employed, and every man fears where it will light, being not a little terrified with a precedent of dangerous consequence, of one Robarts of Cornwall or Devonshire, whose father, an obscure fellow, dying exceeding rich, they say, by long use of interest, there was a privy seal sent unto him for 20,000*l.* with intimation that, whereas by law the King could seize upon all gotten by these usurious courses, he was of his clemency content to borrow this sum without interest. In conclusion the man was brought to lend 12,000*l.* to be repayed by 1,200*l.* a year."—Birch, i. 446. Whichever of these stories be true, Mr. Robartes was knighted on the 11th November in this year; created a Baronet 1621, and Baron Robartes 1625; and he doubtlessly, as was the practice of the age, paid handsomely for each of these honours. His father was John Robartes, a merchant of Truro.

This 24. of November, by a shippe of London thatt came frome the bottome of the Streyghts, itt is reported that the Hollanders men of warre (whom the Estates do employ to serve vppon those pirattes) came before the port of Tunis, and sent to the Kinge requiringe him to send vnto them such Hollanders as had bene latelye taken att sea and made slaves, or ells they would take there revendge vppon all the Turkes they should meet withall, wherevppon the slaves were sent vnto them. I dowt whether this report be trew, because since the first divulginge of itt itt hathe nott beene seconded. From thence they passed to Angier, and of that kinge they made the like demaund, who nott onlye refused there desire, but sent them a raylinge and scornfull answere. The Hollanders ridinge in the port and ready to set sayle to be gone, att the very instant two Turkishe pirattes came bearinge in; the Hollanders assayled them, tooke the shippes, and, in view of the towne, hanged all the Turkes vppon the yardes armes, and so departed. The Kinge of Spayne (whose continent nott longe since hathe bene invaded, and villadges nott far frome Malaga ransacked, and divers of his subiects carried away slaves,) is nott so forward to suppress these pirattes as is to be wished. Of any Christian prince itt most concernes him, and itt is a wonder vnto me thatt the Kinge and Counsayle of Spayne do nott take itt more at hart, for yf itt be suffered to grow on, the suppressinge of these common enemies to all commerce will be no less difficult in these our dayes then the Bellum Piraticum was to the Romans, which was nott the least of Pompeis triumphes.

In this moneth Sir William Seager, Garter Principall Kinge att Arms, was knighted; and before him, at Allhallow tide last, Sir Richard St. George, Norroy King att Armes, was also knighted. Clarentiaulx Camden, inferior to nether of theme in abilitie or learninge, hathe nott yett put out his toppe sayles.

Geve me leave a little to digress frome the nature of a gazette, and fall into a discourse nott unworthye the consideration. The passage through the Vaygats vnto Pechora in the Samoydes countrye (subiects to the Emperour of Moscovie) our Englishe marchants have

Geographical remarks.

often proved in the tyme of the yere to be open.   The Russes, yerely, from St. Nicolas trade as farre as the mouth of the river of Ob, and retourne, the which we may allso do.   This great river of Ob (as I understand) on ether banke, even from the mouthe of itt unto the great lake from whence itt springeth,[a] is possessed by the Moscovite, and in places convenient castles are seated and gvarded for the saftie of those which trade vppon thatt river.   Betwene the rivers of Indus and Ganges and the Ob there is no great extent of land, why may not then the commodities of Mogulls countrie, Persia, and the kingdoms adiacent (yf the the rivers of Indus or Ganges be navigable as the Ob is) be brought vnto us with more ease, muche more saftie and lesse charge, then by the tedious and dangerous navigation now practised.   I leave itt to your consideration, and yf the proiect be feasible (whereof in my opinion there is little dowbt) you may do your countrye good service, and winne honnour vnto yourselfe in beinge the proiector of so good a worke.   The greatest impediment which I conceve is the passage vppe the foresaid rivers and the land travell betwene them and Ob, for down that river vnto the sea I amme informed thatt the passage is easie and safe.   Itt will be worthe youre care to learne whatt you may of the Indus, and of the nations betwene it and the Ob.

" The Grace of God of London," of the burden of 180 tonnes, which put to sea from the coast of Spayne (loaden with Spanishe commodities) the 28 of September, is thought to be taken [by] the Turkishe pirattes within the mouthe of the Streygthes: more of the like misfortunes we must expect by those infidells.

December.—Sorrowfull newes from Elbine,[b] within the Sound, is December. come to the companye of Eastland marchants in London, by the General news. breakinge of a Scottishman's sonne borne there, who had in his possession of Englishe goodes to the valew of 80,000[ll]. and vpwards: by this bankrout Alderman Cockayne alone hathe lost, as I amme in-

[a] It is presumed that Lake Dzaisang (Lat. 46, N., Long, 84, E.), the source of the Irtisch, the chief western branch of the Obi, is here meant.   [b] In Prussia.

formed, above 1,000*l*.[a]   Allso there is another broken att Hambourge
(as itt is thought) for a farre greater somme, but the truthe is nott
yett exactlye knowne; in the mean tyme our marchants are perplext.

The Kinge att Newmarkett hathe knighted Huntingdon Colbye[b]
and Ferdinando Knightlie,[c] who served the last Lord Threasorer;[d]
both of them were knowne vnto you.

The first of this moneth the Ladye Cheeke[e] (att her house by
Charinge Cross) died, beinge very neere 100 years of age.

The 8. Doctor Leake,[f] brother to Mr. Secretarye Leake, and
Doctor Bayllye,[g] who preacheth a piquant sermon (as itt was vnder-
stood) agaynst the Earle of Northampton in his lyfe tyme, were consecrated bushopps att Lambethe, the one of Bathe and Wells, the
other of Bangor.

The 9, The Ladie Harrington[h] beganne her iourney towards
Heddleberge, to attend her Highnesse, which she vndertooke by
the Electrise intreatie, and the Kinges comandment: towards her
chardges she was imprested out of the Exchequer 5,000*l*.   I ame
afrayed thatt (as her husband did) she will there end her dayes.

---

[a] William Cockaine, an eminent London merchant, Sheriff 1609, and soon afterwards
elected an Alderman. He was the Chief of the New Company of Merchant Adventurers,
which gave the King a great banquet at Alderman Cockaine's house on 22nd June in this
year, on which occasion the alderman was knighted with the city sword. He was Lord
Mayor 1619, and died 1626. Dr. Donne preached his funeral sermon

[b] He was of the Suffolk family of Colbys, and was knighted on 23rd November. He
died abroad, and letters of administration were granted to his sister Mary Cópuldick, on
19th May, 1618.—Prerog. Court, Acts of Administration, 170.

[c] Fifth son of Sir Richard Knightley, of Fawsley, co Northampton. He was a Captain
of Foot in Holland, and was living in 1645, but died unmarried.

[d] The Earl of Salisbury.

[e] Mary, daughter of R. Hill, Esq. and widow of Sir John Cheke, Tutor of King
Edward VI. After the death of Sir John Cheke, she married Henry Mac-Williams, of
Ireland. She died on 30th November, 1616, and was buried at St. Martin's-in-the-Fields.

[f] Arthur Lake, (not Leake,) Dean of Worcester.

[g] Dr. Lewis Bayley was a native of Carmarthen. Died 1632. He was the author
of " The Practice of Piety."

[h] Anne, daughter and sole heir of John Keilway, Esq. Surveyor of the Court of Wards
and Liveries, and widow of John first Lord Harrington. Lord and Lady Harrington were

About the later end of this last monethe three gentlemen of the Innes of the Court were slayne in duell: one of them called Christmas had quarrell with the other two, whose names were Burton and Bellingham; they agreed to fight beyond the seas nott farre frome Callice: Christmas tooke for his second little Arthur Wingfield,[a] who had bene the Countesse of Bedford's page, and first slew Burton, and after Bellingham tooke his turne and was likewise slayne, but not without revendge, for he slew Christmas. Arthur Wingfield came home to bringe the newes of the duell, there beinge no cause for him to draw his sword.

The Lord Rich [b] is maried to the Ladie St.Paul, of Lincolneshire; she was daughter of the Chief Justice Wray.[c]

Monsieur Dedigueres, the Mareshall of France, is gone into Piemont in the ayde of the Duke of Savoy with 12,000 Frenche foote, and 1,200 horse.

It is sayed that the Duke de Nemours is reconciled to his cosen the Duke of Savoy.

---

highly esteemed by King James I., and were entrusted with the care of the Princess Elizabeth. (Granger.) They accompanied her to Germany in 1613 on her marriage, and Lord Harrington died at Worms on the 24th August in that year. Lord Carew's fears were not altogether groundless. Lady Harrington was seized with a dangerous sickness in France on her return from the court of Heidelburg in May 1619, (Birch, ii. 167,) but nevertheless reached London on the 29th of that month, when, we are told, crowds assembled in Bishopsgate to witness her arrival. (S.P.O. Dom. Corr. vol. cix. 59.) On the 8th June she was very ill, (ibid. 62,) after which we trace no further notice of her. (See note [d], p. 11.)

[a] Arthur Wingfield was a younger son of Sir Edward Wingfield, of Kimbolton, co. Huntingdon, by Mary, fifth daughter of Sir James Harrington, of Exton, co. Rutland. He was therefore the Countesse of Bedford's first cousin. He was also a kinsman of the Lord Carew, by common descent from Bridget, daughter and heir of Sir John Wiltshire, and wife, successively, of Sir Richard Wingfield, of Kimbolton, K.G., and Sir Nicholas Harvey. He was killed in a duel 1st December, 1617. See under that date.

[b] Robert, third Lord Rich, created Earl of Warwick 1618. Died 1618.

[c] Frances, daughter of Sir Christopher Wray, Lord Chief Justice, and widow of Sir George St.Paul, of Snarford, co. Lincoln, knighted 1607, created a Baronet in 1611. Died s.p.

CAMD. SOC.   K

Sir John Swinerton,[a] that was Mayor of London, is dead.

Doctor Parry,[b] the Bishoppe of Worcester, (who was a good, godlye, and learned prelate,) is dead: God grant a good successor.

The 16. the Archbishop of Spalato,[c] in Dalmatia, a reverend and learned Bishoppe, detestinge the Romishe tradition and discipline, came to London, and means to spend the rest of his dayes in England; he is a man of great estimation, of many yeres, and quited his prelacye for conscience' sake.

Every day we hear of our shippes taken in the Levant by the Turkishe piratts, and very latelye they have taken two marchant shipps of London.

The 22. Sir Thomas Edmonds,[d] the Ambassador Lidgier in France, was att Whitehall sworne a Counceller; and the same day the Vicecount Wallingford[e] resigned his office of Threasorer of the

[a] He was Alderman and Sheriff of London at the King's accession, and was knighted with the other aldermen at Whitehall 26th July, 1603. In 1612 he was Lord Mayor, and entertained the King at a grand banquet in Merchant Taylors' Hall. Chamberlain say, that " he was not altogether so great and rich a man as he was held and made shew of."—Birch, i. p. 448.

[b] Dr. Henry Parry was of Corpus Christi college, Oxford, and Greek Reader there; made Dean of Chester 1605, Bishop of Gloucester 1607, translated to Worcester 1610.

[c] Mark Antony de Dominis, Archbishop of Spalato, in Dalmatia, quarrelled with the Pope and renounced Popery. He received many marks of the King's favour, but soon retracted all he had said and written, and returned to Rome. Gregory XV. received him courteously, but his successor, Urban VIII., threw him into the Inquisition.

[d] Son of Thomas Edmondes, of Plymouth. He was employed on many embassies, which he executed with great wisdom and fidelity. Knighted 1603. Chamberlain, writing to Carleton on 4 January, 1617, says:—" Sir Thomas Edmondes was made Controller, and had the white staffe delivered him the first howre he saw the King, and dothe execute the place with courage and authoritie enough, but they say he doth somewhat too much flourish and fence with his staves, whereof he hath broken two alredy, (not at tilt), but stickling at the playes this Christmas. I wish him all honour and good successe, and specially a fayre young rich widow lately fallen, Sir Fraunces Anderson's lady, yf he have a mind to her, and, which is more *rebus sic stantibus*, niece to the Lord Villiers by his sister Sir John Butler's lady." (S.P.O. Dom. Corr. xc. 8.) He succeeded Lord Wotton as Treasurer 1618. Died 1639.

[e] William Knollys Baron Knollys, created Viscount Wallingford 14th November 1616 (see p. 55), and Earl of Banbury 1626, K.G. Died 1632.

Householld to the Lord Woottan,[a] and the Comptroller's staffe was delivered to Sir Thomas Edmonds.

The same day allso the marchants of the Levant Companye pre- Levant Com-
pany. ferred a petition to the Councell Bord humblye beseechinge the lords to move his Majestie to write his lettres in there favour to the Grand Signor, for they find themsellves iniured by the Vizier Bassa, who hathe imprisoned there principall factor Mr. Arthur Garraway, sonne to Sir William Garraway,[b] constraynes them to pay new impositions, andthreatens them to pay head money as the Greekes and Jewes do, so as they are in some feare of a confiscation; and, in briefe, the Turkes beginne to breake all the conditions of the contract betwene us and them. The ground of all this trouble arisethe from the spoyles and robberies committed (as the Turkes alleadge) by our marchants vppon the Grand Signor's subiects in the East Indies, whereof daylie complaints and informations comes to Constantinople. Besides they complayned of robberies and piracies done vppon vs in the Levant by Turkishe pirattes, whereof nethir att Angiere, Tvnis, or Constantinople they finde no remedie. What will be the yssue of these troubles (which threatens the overthrow of our trade in the Levant,) tyme will produce.

In Irland the Lord Deputie[c] proceeds roundlye with the cittie recu- Persecutions in
Ireland. sants: he beganne with Dublin, where some of the principall officers of the cittie were imprisoned, fined, and disfranchised. The like is done in the other citties, so as there is above fourscore of the best sort of cittizens now in prison; the like course is held with the jurors who would nott present knowne and obstinatt recusants. Yf this course do holld, which for my part I wishe, the prisons in Irland willbe to little for the delinquents. In the end itt will fall out thatt there chartres willbe resumed, and worthelye, for in corpo-

---

[a] Edward Wotton, created Baron Wotton 1603.

  Knighted 1615. Chamberlain says, "Old Garraway, the chief of the Customers, was knighted on Sunday at Theobalds, as well for other good services as for giving security to the aldermen for the coal money, without which they made much difficulty to be brought to it."

[c] Sir Oliver St.John.

ratt townes in that realme no magistratts canne be found that will
ether take the oathe of supremicye or alleadgeance, which is a sufficient cause of forfayture of there priviledges; but when there townes
shallbe reduced into villadges, I am of opinion they willbe more
conformable and submit themsellves as good subiects ought to do.
God I hope will prosper these good beginnings, which tends onlye
to his prayse and glorye, and to the assurance of obedience vnto his
Majestie.

A Prophecy.   Profetia mandata dal Nuntio di N. S. in Francia all' Illustrissimo
Cardinal Borghese, la quale é stata trovata nel riuevare un fonda-
mento d'vn pilastro vna Casetta di marmo, nella chieza di S.
Dionigi, scritta in lingua Ebraica.

1620. Bellum magnum in tota Italia.

1622. Pastor non erit.

1623. Ira Dei super vniversam terram.

1624. A paucis cognoscetur Christus.

1625. Resurget magnus vir.

1626. Africa ardebit, et luna scaturiet sanguinem.

1627. Terræmotus magnus in toto orbe.

1628. Evropa, Africa, et Asia trepidabunt.

1629. Infideles trinum et unum Deum cognoscent.

1630. Extinguentur Lumina, et unus Pastor et unum ovile.

Of this idle prophetie you may beleeve what you list; for my
owne particular I geve no more creddit vnto them then vnto Las
patrannas dellas mugeres viejas.[a]

Foreign news.   The newes from Savoy is thatt the Duke of Savoy, by the ayde
of Mareschall de Digeneres, and since his reconcilliation with the
Duke of Nemours his kinsman, hathe Savoy quiet, prospers in Piemont, and now makes an offensive warre agaynst the Kinge of
Spayne in the Duchye of Millan.

In the Low Countries feare of new troubles so affrightethe the
natives on ether side as the gentlemen of the Vnited Provinces
make sale of there lands within the Archduke's dominions, and the

---

[a] A similar prophecy, slightly varying in respect to some of the years, is recorded,
under the date 1621, in Yonge's Diary, p. 38.—Camd. Soc.

like is done by the Count Aremberge[a], and others which have lived
in the sayed provinces; for you must vnderstand when the truce was
concluded the lords and gentlemen on ether side had the full vse
and profitt of there inheritances restored vnto them.   His Majestie
is daylye wowed[b] by the Frenche and the Spanish Kinges for to
marry his sonne, our hopefull prince, vnto a French madame, or a
Spanishe infanta: the Kinge our master deliberates, and so conceales
his intention as no man knows vppon which of them the lot will fall.

The Duke of Vrbin is shortlye to marry with the third sister of
the Duke of Florence.[c]   He hathe of late beene at Florence, where
he was magnificentlye intertayned, but the marriage defferred vntill
the great Dukc's[d] retourne frome Lorretto, whether he is gone to pay
a vow he made in a great sickness which he had, and duringe his
absence the Duchesse daylye goes frome churche to churche, prayinge
for his safe retourne.

Frances Anslow,[e] brother to the Queen's servant Mrs. Anslow, and General news.
heretofore servant to the Lord Chichester, knighted this last sommer,
is now a joynt Secretarye in Irland with Sir Dudlye Norton, and
consequentlye a councellor of thatt realme.

Mr. Doctor Burgess,[f] the silenst minister, is now agayne permitted

[a] John de Ligne, Prince of Barbançon and Count of Aremberg, Ambassador in England
from the Archduke of Austria 1603.

[b] To wowe, to woo. (See Halliwell.)

[c] Claudia, daughter of Ferdinand I. Grand Duke of Florence, and sister of Cosmo II.,
born 1604 ; married Frederick Ubaldus, Prince of Urbino (1621,) who dying in 1623,
she married Leopold, Archduke of Austria. Died 1632.—Moreri.

[d] Cosmo II., Duke of Florence 1608-21.   He was a very sickly prince, and died 28
February 1621. His Duchess was Mary Magdalen, daughter of Charles Archduke of
Austria, whom he married 19th October, 1608. She died 1631.—Anderson.

[e] Sir Francis Annesley, son of Robert Annesley, one of the undertakers of Munster,
knighted 1616. Previously to this date he had held several important offices in Ireland.
(Liber Munerum Hiberniæ.)   In 1620 he was created a Baronet in that country, and
was afterwards raised to the peerage as Baron Mountnorris and Viscount Valentia. Died
1660. His sister was Lady of the Bedchamber to the Queen.

[f] Dr. John Burgess. In 1604 he gave great offence to the King, and was imprisoned,
for certain remarks made in a sermon on the graciousness of princes and the impartiality
of their favours; which he admitted were made because the people murmured at the want

to preache, and reades the lecture in the parishe without Bishoppes-
gate.

French news. Temines, the new made Mareschall of France, is now discharged
frome the command of the Bastill, and the same is committed to
Mareschall de Ancre, of whose care to keep the Prince of Conde there
is no doubt to be made.

The Earl of
Arundell re-
ceived into the
Church of Eng-
land. This Christmas day the Erle of Arundell receved the communion
in Whitehall, and there is no doubt but he is as firmelye settled in
our religion as may be wished, which is a good leadinge example to
other of our noblemen, which are refractorie to conformitie.[a]

Difference with
the Netherlands
respecting dyed
and dressed
cloths. Ever since your departure from England there hathe beene a great
difference between vs and the United Provinces, about our Englishe
clothes, for they will not permitt the sellinge of our clothes which
are died and dressed in England in there estate, and to manifest there
dislike, they published an edict prohibitinge vppon payne of confiscation any of our clothes to come into there portes; we on the contrarye are as resolute to enforce them to buy our dressed and died
clothes, or ells to remove our residence at Middlebourge. This hathe
reseved sundry consultations at the Councell Bord, where the Kinge
hathe sundry tymes bene personallye with his lords; but yet the
busines is not ended. For the better composinge of this great worke,

of these qualities in the King. He also made some unpalatable observations on religion,
shewing a puritan tendency. (S.P.O. Dom. Corr. vol. viij. 85.) In 1617 he was permitted
to preach at Paul's Cross. (Ibid. vol. xcij. 88.)

  [a] Chamberlain, writing to Carleton on 4th January, 1617, says, " The Earle of Arundell
receaved the Communion on Christmas day in the Kinges Chappell, where there were two
excellent sermons made that day by the Bishop of Winchester and the Bishop of Ely,
and a third that afternoone in Powles by the Bishop of London, and I heard the Bishop
of Rochester as much commended at his parish of St. Giles without Creplegate. Yester-
day there fell a great mischaunce to the Earle of Arundell by the burning of his house
(built and left him by the Earle of Northampton) at Greenwich, where he likewise lost a
great deale of houshold stuffe and riche furniture, the fury of the fire being such that
nothing could be saved. No doubt the Papists will ascribe and publish yt as a punishment
for his dissembling or falling from them." (S.P.O. Dom. Corr. vol. xc. 8.) Sir Horace
Vere, writing to Carleton on the 8th January, says, " My Lord of Arundell hath receaved
the sacrament with the Kinge this Christmas, and, as I hear, in his discourses with his Majestie is sharp agaynst the Papists, which is a good argument of his synceritie."—Ib. 11.

which troubles bothe vs and them, they send there agents hether, which are daylie expected; in the mean tyme our merchants labour with the Archduke [a] to have a place of residence in his territories, which is like enoughe to take effect.

To avoyd bothe your trouble and myne, I leave you to the report of the Englishe factors, which do now go to Suratt, who cane at lardge discourse vnto you the reasons of the differences between vs, which arisethe onelye about matter of proffit, for the dyinge and dressinge of clothes in England takes from them the mayntenance of 600,000 persons who gayned there livinges by the dressinge and dyinge of Englishe clothe, which we are desirous should be kept within the realme for the reliefe of our poore people. Yf you call to mynde the new companye of marchaunts adventurers which were erected before you lefte England, who vndertooke to carry no clothes but dressed and dyed out of the realme, you will quicklye conceve the cause of the difference betweene vs and the Hollanders; the progression in which busines will aske a lardge discourse and a better relater than myselfe, but when it is concluded and ended, I will nott forgett to lett you know the conclusion.

Sir Walter Raleghe hathe built a goodlye shipp of 500 tonnes; in this monethe she was lanched, and is called the "Destinye." God graunt her to be no lesse fortunatt vnto her owner than is wished by me! In Februarie next he purposes to sett sayle towardes his golden myne, whereof he is extremely confident. $\quad$ Sir Walter Raleigh's Expedition.

The allarme of his iorney is flowne into Spayne, and, as he tells me, sea forces are prepared to lye for him, but he is nothinge appalled with the report, for he will be a good fleet and well manned; the number and names of his shipps, captens, and forces,* you shall receve with these. I amm sure he will be able to land 500 men, which is a competent armye to performe any exploite vppon the con-

---

* *In the margin.* This promise I cannot perform untill Sir W. R. be nearer his departure. In my next I will not forgett itt.

[a] Archduke of Gratz, see note [c] p. 49.

tinent of America, the Spaniards (and especiallye about Orinoque) beinge so poorelye planted as they are.

The King resolved to visit Scotland.

The Kinge is resolved this next springe to visite Scotland. Vppon the 15 day of Marche he beginnes his iorney: the gistes ᵃ are alreadie sett down, bothe for his lodginges in goinge and retourninge. The sommer he will spend there; and, before bucke tyme be throughlie past he meanes to make us happie with his presence. Least some alteration should happen, I do yett forbeare to send you the list of the noblemen and others of quallitie which are appoynted to attende him in this longe progresse; but I amm confident that the iorney will holld. His gistes comminge and goinge throughe England I send you with these; his gistes in Scotland we know nott.

A coat of arms granted to the common hangman.

The 28th of this monethe the Kinge was informed that Garter the Principall Kinge att Armes had geven a coate of armes vnto one Gregorie Brandon the hangman of London, whereatt his Majestie was highly offended, commandinge the Lords Marshalls to examyne the truthe. The fact was proved to be trew, for the armes was produced vnder the seale of the office, and testified by Garter's subscription; but in the procuringe of itt he was muche abused, for one came vnto him with the armes readie paynted in parchement, and an attestation formallye drawne fitt for his subscription in dew forme, sayinge that this Gregorie Brandon was a marchant of good abilitie then in Spayne, and thatt he was descended frome one Brandon that sometymes was Mayor of London. Garter, findinge that the armes was belonginge to the familye of Brandons thatt had beene dwellinge in London, and supposinge (as he was informed) thatt this hangman had been trewlye a merchant in Spayne, attested that Gregorie Brandon might lawfully beare the coate which was brought vnto him. This abuse was contrived by Yorke Heraldᵇ to draw Garter into disgrace. The conclusion I think will fall out thatt the one will be punished for foolerie, and the other for knaverye,

---

ᵃ The gests or stages of the progress.

ᵇ Ralph Brook, a man of such infamous character that he was several times upon the point of being dismissed from his office. Died 1625.

of which faûlts they are gviltie. In the meane tyme the hangman
is now a gentleman, which he never dreamed of. Since the hearinge
of the cause Garter and Yorke were bothe committed prisoners by the
Lords Marshalls to the Marshaltie, where they yet remayne.

I tolld you thatt nott many dayes past Monsieur Temines had Marshal Temines re-
the government of the Bastill in Paris taken from him and com- moved from
mitted to the care of Marshall d'Ancre; the cause of his displacinge the government of the Bastile.
arose out of jealousie conceved thatt the Prince of Conde had gayned
some interest in him. The resolution beinge taken (to remove him
without danger or noyse) he was sent for by the Queene Mother,
who was in the Lovvre. In his absence he left his sonne to supplye
his office, who by devise was drawne out of the Bastill to walk
ether in the garden, or some such place: he was no sooner out of
the gates but the drawbridge was pulled vppe and a comission read
for the placinge of the Marshall d'Ancre in thatt chardge. The
Marshall Temines, ashamed to tarry in Paris any longer with such a
scorne, *is gone discontented from the Court*,* and the vniversal discontentment throughout all France bathe so farre enlarged itt sellfe as all
men are of opinion that shortlye a bitter warre will ensue. The Duke
of Gvise hathe carried himselfe so indiscreetlye betweene the Queene
and the Princes as thatt he is trusted by nether side, yett he
remaynes in the Court with as many discontents as his hart cane beare.

In Aix or Aquis-grane the Emperor's comissioners have pro- General news.
ceeded secretlye agaynst them of the religion, and of late some have
bene executed for matters of religion onelye, some others banished
and confiscated, and very many grievouslye fined. Most of the
confiscations have bene geven to the Jesuites.

In the Low Countries, I meane the Vnited Provinces, the estates
are muche troubled about the multiplicitie of religions which daylye
increases amongst them, for the reformation whereof commissioners
are appoynted; but whatt will be the yssue God knowes.

---

* To geve him some satisfaction the Queene hathe made his sonne the capten of her
gvard, and with fayre words hathe so bewitched the old man as thatt he did nott abandon the Court.

Count John of Nassau, who longe since hathe embarqued his regiment against the Archduke Ferdinand, is hetherto stayed by contrarye wyndes, and sicknes is fallen amongst them; which yf itt increase itt is feared thatt the designe will breake.

A riche shippe of the Netherlands thatt tooke in her ladinge (att Cipres) in the bottom of the Levant, and beinge safelye arryved at Amsterdam, by misfortune was fired, no man knows how, so as very little of the merchandize was saved.

This last day of December the matter of clothe beinge dealt in by the Kinge and his counsayle, itt is found, apparentlye, thatt the new companye of marchant adventurers are not able to performe the vndertakinge which they promised for the dyinge and dressinge of our clothes within the realme, where vppon the olde companye are like to be agayne established, butt whatt will be there conditions is nott yett agreed vppon: a few dayes will drive this busines to an yssue.

French news. The Duke of Espernon continewes in armes agaynst the Rochellers, but we do nott heare of any great attempt performed on ether part.

The Duke of Nevers, to assvre (in this vncertayne tyme in France) a little walled towne of his vppon the borders of Lorrayne (the name whereof I have forgotten*), put a garrison into itt. The Queen demanded the towne of him to place a garrison of hers in the same; which he refusinge, she corrupted his men; his garrison is displaced, and the Queenes gvard keepes itt for her vse, which bathe so discontented the Duke as now he is ioyned with the other princes, who are dispersed into there severall governments, preparinge, as itt is sayed, for a new warre: few or none of the great men of France comes to the court.

The Duke of Savoy hathe recovered all his places in Piemont frome the Spaniards, except the towne of St. German.

1617.
January.   *Januarye.*—The 3. the Erle of Northampton's newe-built house

---

* St. Monehute, see p. 80.

att Greenwiche (by the negligence of servants) is burned all (but the gallerye) to the ground, wherein the Erle of Arundell (whose house it was,) loste a greate part of his household stuffe, which was of greate valew.[a]

The 4. the new Companie of Marchant Adventurers were dis- New Company
solved, and the olld company was restored, who promise to effect the   of Merchant
Adventurers
dressinge and dyinge of clothes within the realme, which beinge   dissolved, and
the Old Com-
performed, one of the best workes thatt ever was thought vppon   pany restored.
(for the commonwealthe) will be established; God graunt thatt I may
live to see itt l [b]

The 5. the Vicecount Villiers was at Whitchall created Erle of Buckingham; the Erle of Montgomerie carried his robes, the Erle of Dorset his sword, the Duke of Lennox, as Erle of Richmond, his cappe, the Lord Admiral his coronet, and supported by the Erle of Suffolk Lord Threasurer, and the Erle of Worcester Lord Privie Seale.

The last newes of France is that the Marshall d'Ancre's onely French news.
daughter is dead, with whom he offered 800 thousand crownes in marriage. It is sayed the Duke of Espernon's second sonne, Monsieur La Vallette, shall be made a Duke of France, thatt his third sonne shall be a cardinall. But I conceve them to be but ayrie reports.

The Queene, as is reported, entends to send some companies to do some exploite vppon the Duke of Nevers, against whom she hathe conceved an implacable displeasure. Most of the princes of France are assembled at Soyssons, which is under the government of the Duke de Mayne, where itt is thought thatt some great desseygne will be concluded, the yssue whereof will shortlye appeare.

---

[a] See note [a], p. 70.

[b] Chamberlain writing to Carleton on 4th January says, " After so long and vehement debating, the Old Companie of Marchant Adventurers is to be set up again, and this day theyre charter to be restored to them, but with what conditions and limitations I have not yet learned." S. P. O. Dom. Corr. vol. xcii. 85.

The report goes thatt the Kingdome of Navarre and the signories of Bearne and Bigorre are to be vnited and annexed, as Brettagne is, vnto the crowne of France; which is a great blow to the Duke of Rohan's title, who is heyre in remaynder vnto the children of Kinge Henry the 4. and geves fuell to his former discontentments.

General news. We have newes of the Lord Rosse's safe arryval att Lisbone, and thatt a fewe dayes before his cominge thether the West Indie Fleete (enforced by fowle wether) came into thatt porte richlye laden, to the valew of 20 millions of ducatts, whereof 9 millions in silver and gold was presentlye (sent) overland vnto Madrid. Allso att the same tyme the East Indie Fleet arrived there, which att no tyme hathe beene seene that bothe the fleetes should meet in one harborough.

News from
Germany. The report frome Collen, in Germanie, is that the second sonne of Spayne [a] is to marrye with the second daughter of France,[b] but in England there is no suche newes, nether do I think itt to be likelye.

The Frenche companies servinge the Estates have nott received for 12 monethes past any wages out of France, which makes the Netherlanders conceve thatt the Queene entends nott to continew them in thatt service, as hetherto they have beene.

For the Kinge of Spayne leveis of mariners are made in the Archduke's dominions, and great wages are proffered vnto all suche Hollanders as will serve him: to whatt end they are levied is yett vn-knowne, but supposed to be agaynst the Turkishe pirattes, and to man his East Indie Fleete, now in settinge forthe, which consists of 7 or 8 great gallions and divers smaller vessels; but itt is thought thatt out of the Vnited Provinces few or none will serve him.

There is a great mortallitie of souldiours in the regiment which are aboord their shippes to go for Venice under Count John of Nassau, and to supplie there roomes others are daylie levied: yf they depart nott the sooner the designe is in danger to be broken.

---

[a] Charles, son of Philip III., born 1607, died 30 July, 1632.

[b] Christina, daughter of Henry IV., born 1606, married Amadeus Duke of Savoy 1619, died 1663.

The Queene to assure the Isle of France, which is the Duke de
Maynes government, hathe put all the tenible places within the
same into the handes and charge of the Marshall de Ancre, which
increases the discontent of the grandes.

This 16. of Januarye, Sir Thomas Smithe, with certayne of the Roe's letters.
East Indie Companie, presented to the Lords of the councell the
coppie of a lettre of yours, dated att Asmore in Februarye last, and
sent overland to Aleppo, where the English Consull opened the
same, and sent the aforesayed coppie by the next messendger to Sir
Thomas Smithe. But your lettres to his Majesty, to the lordes of the
counsell and others, were delivered (as Sir Thomas Smithe tolld me)
to Mr. Porie [a] (our olld acquayntance) by the Consull of Aleppo,* who
is nott yett come into England, but daylie expected, whose deathe long
since was constantlye affirmed to be at Constantinople. In this coppie
presented vnto the lords, there is a proiect of yours, for the openinge
of a trade in Persia; the lords like so well of itt, and the marchants _{Proposed trade}
so willinge to finde itt, as thatt it is concluded thatt a tryall thereof _{with Persia.}
shall be made; further particularities I need nott write, for Sir
Thomas Smithe must necessarilye acquaynt you with itt, for you must
be the chiefest actor in the performance of the worke, and vnto his
lettres I referre you. Since there is suche a madnes in England as
thatt we cannott endure our homemade clothe, but must needes be
clothed in silke, itt cannott be gayne-sayed but the silkes bought att
the first hand is the best husbandrye, and therefore to settle a trade
in Persia (*prima facie*) is bothe convenient and commodious; but
nothinge cane be so cleerelye good thatt ·bathe not itts exception,

---

* The consull at Aleppo sent your pacquett to the Ambassador att Constantinople, who
sent them by Mr. Porye for England.

---

[a] Mr. John Pory was educated at Cambridge, where he took the degree of **M.A.** in
1610. He was a man of extensive travel, and of great talent and general information as to
what was going on jn the political world both at home and abroad. Notwithstanding his
habits of intemperance, he seems to have been on intimate terms with many of the most
eminent of his contemporaries, to whom he often performed the office of secretary. Died
1635.

and therefore (in my opinion) there are three obiections worthye the
consideration: the first is the least, the other two of more importance.   My first obiection is the port of Jasques,ª which to my
seeminge (according to Mercator's description nott haveinge any por-
table river) is inconvenient ether to having the commodities of the
countrye vnto itt, or to vent ours into the land.   But hereof you
may bettre informe your sellfe then we canne, liuinge so remote
from itt, and itt may be thatt a convenient port to our marchants
likinge may be found, wherefore I will no longer insist vppon this
obiection.

My second and third obiections are meerlye matter of state, which
will require mature consideration.

In December last, (as in the Gazette of thatt moneth you
may see,) I related vnto you how yll our men are vsed att Constantinople, and as farre as I canne judge there yll usage is
liklier to continew then receve amends; yf we shall settle a
trade in Persia, how farre forth the Grand Signor may be irritated
to the confiscation of all the Englishe marchants goodes (throughout his dominions) is to be feared, whereby the kingdome shall
receve great damage, and a profitable trade destroyed.   Here
vnto itt may be answered that, so longe as we shall demeane
ourselves in a peaceable manner towards the Turkes, thatt there
is no cause why he should take offence att itt.   This reason
amonge Christians is so prevalent and just as thatt itt would geve
sufficient satisfaction, but how itt may worke in the hart of a Turke,
who governs his actions by no other rule then by his will, for my
owne part I amme dowbtfull.   The third obiection is how we may
draw vnto vs the silkes of Persia, which are onelye solld (as I have
beene informed) for readie money: yf they cannott be gotten by no
other meanes, thatt trade onlye will exhaust the threasure of the
realme, for, yf I be nott deceved, 600,000^{li}. will scarcely be able to
drive thatt trade.   Your judgement gayned by your present em-

ª Jask, in the Sea of Oman.

ployment is bettre able to resolve this dowbt then myne of so little experience, wherefore I referre my sellfe vnto itt, prayinge you in your next to signifie your opinion vnto me in all the three obiections. Vnderstandinge thatt the East Indie fleet is ready to fall downe the river, I am enforced to end this gazzette, which will be more troublesome for you to reade then itt was for me to write, for, ever since Januarie 1615 itt hathe beene in writinge, which course I do wishe you to observe in your lettres vuto me, and then I shall be sure to have longe lettres, good discourse, and store of novellties, every thinge of those partes beinge rare vnto vs. God prosper you in your employment with no less happines than your owne hart desires, and rest assured thatt you shall never fayle to the prayers, services, and love, of

Your L. most affectionatt trew frend,

G. CAREW.

Savoy, this 18th of Januarye, 1616.

Thatt you may know how the affayres of the kingdome hathe passed since your departure I do send you two of Mercurius Gallobelgier's editions, and the manifest made by the Archbishop of Spalato, wherein he geves reasons for his defection frome the Churche of Rome; and so once agayne I pray God for my Lord Ambassador's saftie in the Indies, and for his safe retourne. Your Lordship may see thatt I have somme creditt with your Mrs., or rather with the best part of yoursellfe, for so itt is rumoured, thoughe by her constantlye denied, but I amme confident itt is so, and for your sake vntill your retourne. I will not fayle to do her all the service I may.

G. CAREW.

Indorsed,
> *From my Lord Carew,*
> 18 *Jan.* 1616.

LETTER IV.[a]

My first lettre vnto you was of the 18. of Aprill, 1615: my
second of the 24. of Januarye *in eodem anno*, and my third and last
before this bare date the 18. Januarye, 1616: the Gazette is longe,
conteyninge 12. sheetes of paper. Whatt this will prove I know
nott, but whether itt happen to be great or small you cannot be
freed from the trouble of readinge an yll hand which will trye youre
pátience.

January.

January 1616.—The Duke of Nevers, in France, was vppon
the 17. of this monethe (*stilo novo*), proclaymed a traytor, which is
an induction to a warre subsequent. Amonge other causes of this
proceedinge agaynst him, these two are the principallest: the first
thatt, beinge trusted in anno 1615 with a competent armye of the
Kinges to have impeached the Prince of Conde in his marche
towards Bourdeaux, when the Kinge was there to receve his Spanishe
wife, he permitted him to pass the Lóyre, beinge in his power (as is
alleaged) for him to have hindered itt; and the second for puttinge
of a garrison into his towne of Saynt Monehute, and deniynge
to receve the Kinges sent thether by the Queene mother, which
afterward (as in my last lettre you may see)[b] he was dispossessed of,
by coruption of his officers. The princes are on all hands preparinge
for the warre, and to quicken there spiritts there hathe beene very
latelye an assassinatt taken, who hathe confessed that he was promised a great reward to have murdered the Duke de Mayne in
Soyssons; he was discovered by one whom he laboured to be a
partie with him in the murder. How these princes will accord
amonge themsellves vpon a chiefe, they will find muche difficultie,
and as yett nether the boddie of the religion nor any good towne is
knowne to stand for them, but when the drum beates itt is thought
they will want no assistance; in the meane tyme itt is reported thatt
within there particular governments they are bold to take uppe the

----

[a] S. P. O. Dom. Corr. vol. xcv. 22.   [b] Page 74.

Kinges rents towards there defence. The Duke of Savoy prospers in Piemont, havinge thrust the Spaniards out of itt, and latelye he hathe taken the bolldnes to make an attempt vppon the Duchie of Myllan, in the which he hathe wonne 4. or 5. good townes.

From Gvernsey I had intelligence thatt in Spayne there is a great fleet in preparinge to the sea, the pilott maior is sayed to be an Englishman; some say itt is for Phillipines, others for Angiere, but those of soundest judgement conceve itt to be for France, in ayde of the Kinge. Itt will nott be longe before we shall see vppon whatt land this clowd will breake.

The newes frome Colleyne is thatt the Duke of Brunswicke [a] refuses News from Cologne. to obaye the decree of the Imperiall Chamber in deliveringe (as he was enioyned) the territorye of Grobenhagen vnto the Duke of Luneburge,[b] and for the assuringe of the same he hathe garrisoned all the best townes and villages within that territorye. The Duke of Luneburge importunes the Commissioners to put the sentence in execution, and hathe allreadie amassed troopes of soldiours to thatt end, which is thought will be the beginninge of a warre in those partes.

The Kinge of Denmarke, as itt is sayed, hathe latelye made great provisions of armes, to the end, as is supposed, to make an attempt vpon Lubecke or Hambourge, and purposeth to build a stronge fort vppon the River of Elbe, requiringe the Hambourgers to permitt 3,000 of his men to passe throughe there towne.

The Vnited Provinces are sendinge of Comissioners into England

[a] Frederick Ulric, Duke of Brunswick Wolfenbuttel. He restored Grubenhagen to the family of Luneburg, 1617.

[b] Christian, second son of William Duke of Brunswick Luneburg. William left seven sons. The brothers resolved not to divide the dukedom, and cast lots who should marry for the purpose of perpetuating the line. The lot fell to George, the sixth brother. They also agreed to reign in succession, one after another, according to seniority. Christian, in accordance with this arrangement, succeeded his brother Ernest 1611. He was made Bishop of Minden 1599, and of Halberstadt 1616, which see he resigned to a son of the King of Denmark 1623. Died 1633.—Anderson.

CAMD. SOC.   M

to treat with his Maiestie about the affayres of Cleves, which was accorded at Xanten.[a]

[The Archdukes will nott leave the Low Countries for the kingdome of Portugall, but are contented to accept of the kingdome of Valentia in Spayne, whether they are to go to be crowned shortlye, and into the Low Countries Don Carlos[b] is to come frome Spayne to governe those dominions.

Certayne companies which are now in garrison in the Duchie of Jvliers are to be sent by the Kinge of Spayne to the ayde of the Archduke Ferdinand agaynst the Venetians, whose places are to be supplied with new levies.]*

The Kinge of Spayne, as is reported, is to marry with the Duke of Florence his sister, and that he will make ether a peace or a long truce with the Turke, and to thatt end a principall Jesuiste is to be employed, thatt he may have the bettre meanes to employ his forces with bettre assurance in Evrope agaynst the Christians with whome he is in warre. Thus farre is the newes from Colleyne, how muche of itt will prove trew tyme will discover.

ews from rance.

The Duke of Nevers hathe put himself into Mazieres, well garnized with horse and foote, and no cost or labour is omitted to fortify the same.

The young Lord of Roxboroghe, the onelye sonne and heyre to the Erle of Roxboroghe, a gentleman of good hope, is latelye dead in France, which is much lamented by his frends, and endangers the continuance of thatt new erected erledome.[c]

Lord Roos in pain.

From Spayne we heare of the Lord Rosses beinge at Madrid. Before he presented himsellfe to the Kinge he was visited by the ambassadors of France, Venice, and Florence; the Dukes of Lerma,[d] Infantadgo,[e]

* Ut dicitur.

---

[a] Xaintonge.

[b] Second son of Philip III. died 1632 ; see note [a], p. 76.   [c] See note [a], p. 31.

[d] Don François Gomez de Sandoval and Roxas, Duke of Lerma. Died 1625. See note [a], p. 59.

[e] Don Inigo Lopez, fifth Duke of Infantado, died 1601, without issue male. His daughter Anne married her uncle Don Roderic de Mendozá. Their daughter Louisa

Vseda,ᵃ Pennaranda, Salinas.ᵇ* The Marquisses of Pomanca, Siete, Yglesias, and Falces, the Erle of Saldanna, the Secretary of State,ᶜ and others. He was receved by the Kinge in his bed-chamber, by the prince· in another roome, and by the princesse in .another. The next day he was visited by the Duke of Vzeda and the Conde de Altamira,ᵈ grandes of Spayne, attended by the Duke of Cea,ᵉ the Marquesses of Pennafiel and SantGerman, and one of the sonnes of the Conde of Altamira. More than this we have nott yett heard of the Lord Rosse.ᶠ

There hathe bene latelye taken within the streyghts foure of our marchants' shipps by Turkishe piratts as they were homewards bound. *General intelligence.*

Our marchants at Constantinople are much troubled for certayne piracies comitted by Ruppa and Franke vppon the Turkes in the bottome of the Levant. They are in service with the Duke of Florence, and dare not retourne into England; neverthelesse, the Turkes require satisfaction frome our marchants for the losses which they have sustayned; and itt is feared thatt they shall be enforced vnto itt, or purchase there peace by excessive bribes. As for the harmes the Turkishe piratts do vnto our nation, no restitution or justice cane be had.

February the 3. the Ladye Lomley died; and, as itt is sayed, *February.*

* The Duke of Salinas is sayed to go shortly to be Viceroy of Portugal. (Writer's note.)

---

married Don Diego Gomez de Sandoval, and from this marriage came Don Roderic Dias de Vivar de Hurtado de Mendoza Sandoval de la Vega et Luna, seventh Duke of Infantado, died in 1657 without issue.—Imhoff, Hist. Ital. et Hispan. Genealog.

ᵃ Don Christoff de Sandoval, Duke of Uzeda, son of the Duke of Lerma ; see note ᵃ, p. 59. Died 1624.—Imhoff.

ᵇ Don Roderic Sarmiento de Silva, Earl of Salinas and Ribadeo, of the celebrated house of Silva, and twentieth Margrave Allenquer. He engaged in a conspiracy against Philip IV., and died a prisoner in the castle of Leon.—Zedler's Universal Lexicon.

ᶜ   de Camara.

ᵈ Don Antoine de Moscoso Ossorio Mendoza and Rojas, seventeenth Comte d'Altamire, created grandee of Spain. Died 1622.—Imhoff.

ᵉ Don François Gomez de Sandoval et Roxas succeeded his grandfather as second Duke of Lerma 1624. Died 1635 s. p. m.—Imhoff. See note ᵃ, p. 59.

ᶠ A letter from Lord Roos to the Earl of Arundel is given in Lodge's Illustrations,

she hathe bestowed the most of her estate and moveables vppon her neece, the Lord Darcye's daughter, and wyfe to Sir Thomas Savadge.*ᵃ

The 4. the Erle of Buckingham att Whitehall was sworne a councellor.

The same day Monsieur La Tour, an ambassador extraordinarye frome the Kinge of France, had his audience att Whitehall.b

The Marques of Cœvre,ᶜ Governour of Laon and Pierrefont, and vnkle to the Duke of Vendosme by his mother, is proclaymed in France a traytor.

News from the Hague.

From the Hage the newes is thatt the Kinge of Poland ᵈ entends to make warre vppon the Kinge of Sweden. He hathe allreadie levied souldiours about Dantzike, and in Liffland, and sent ambassadors to the Archdukes to send him shippes of warre from Dunkerke

---

* The lease which she had of the Lord Lvmlye's lands in the Northe she bathe geven vnto Sir Richard Lvmlye,ᵉ his landes in Sussex vnto her brother the Lord Darcy, which will fall to the Savadges' share.

---

vol. iii. p. 286, wherein his lordship gives an interesting account of his journey to Madrid and reception at Court.

ᵃ Sir Thomas Savage of Rocksavage, Bart., married Elizabeth, daughter and heir of Thomas Lord Darcy of Chiche, created Viscount Colchester, and afterwards Earl Rivers, with remainder to his son-in-law. Sir Thomas died before the Earl in 1635, but his son succeeded his maternal grandfather in the title in 1639.

ᵇ The object of his embassy was to pray James's aid in suppressing the insurrection of the French Princes. Yonge's Diary (Camd. Soc.) p. 32. He was accompanied by a suite of twenty attendants.—S.P.O. Dom. Corr. vol. xc. 39.

ᶜ François Annibal d'Estrees, Marquis Cœuvres, Peer and Marshal of France, Governor of the Isle of France, and of Soissons, Laon, and the Laonois, created Duke of Cœuvres 1648, died 1670. He was brother of Gabrielle d'Estrees mistress of Henry IV. and mother of the Duke of Vendôme. See note ¹, p. 25.

ᵈ Sigismund III., son of John King of Sweden, by Catherine daughter of Sigismund II. King of Poland. He succeeded to the crown of Sweden on the death of his father in 1592; but he and his heirs were excluded upon religious grounds in 1600, the crown of Sweden being conferred on his uncle Charles, who was succeeded in that kingdom by Gustavus Adolphus in 1611.

ᵉ Sir Richard Lumley, great-grandson of Richard, fourth Lord Lumley, and second cousin of John the sixth and last Lord, who selected him for his heir. Created Viscount Lumley in Ireland 1628. He supported the King in the troubles of the next reign, and held a command in the Royal Army in the West under Prince Rupert.

and his other ports, and to send to the Kinge of Denmarke for his leave thatt they may passe the Sound.

The Kinge of Denmarke is amassinge a great fleet, which makes the citties of Lubecke and Hamburghe to arme, fearing thatt the storme may fall vppon them. It is likewise feared thatt the Dukes of Brunswicke and Lvneburge will shortlye fall into open hostillitie.

The Marquis Spinola hathe bought the title which the Count de Lomay [a] (who is of the familye of Mark) pretends vnto the Duchie of Bovillon; and itt is reported thatt he entends to recover the same by force. The Duke of Bovillon to prevent his deseygnes fortifies all his places, and especiall Sedan, and hathe sent vnto his frends in France, the Low Countries and Germany, requiringe there aydes yf necessitie enforce itt. Thus farre the newes of Hage.

The same day that the Erle of Buckingham was sworne a coun- English news. celler Christopher Villiers,[b] his yongest brother, was sworne a Groome of the Kinges Bedchamber in the place of Robin Hay, who, by the resignation of his brother the Lord Hay, is now Master of the Kinges Robes, which is an office of honnour and proffitt.

The Lord Chanceler, loaden with years and affayres, to ease him-sellfe of vnnecessarye busines, hathe resigned vuto the Lord Cham-berlayne [c] his office of Chanceler of Oxford. The Lieutenancye of the countye of Buckinghame not manye monethes past (whereoff as I remember I mentioned in my last letter) he allso resigned to the Erle of Buckingham; and some are of opinion thatt his purpose is by degrees to retire himsellfe, as muche as he may, from all pub-

---

[a] Charles Robert de la Marck, Count of Maulevrier and Lumain, second son of Robert fourth Duke of Bouillon of that house. He assumed the title of Duke of Bouillon after the death, without issue, in 1594, of Charlotte, only daughter of Henry Robert his brother, fifth duke. Charlotte had married Henry de la Tour, Viscount and Marshal Turenne, and carried the dukedom of Bouillon to that family; and, notwithstanding she died without issue, neither the Count de Lumain, nor his posterity, nor Spinola, if he purchased the right, could ever recover the title from the powerful house of Turenne.

[b] Christopher Villiers, third and youngest son of Sir George Villiers by his second wife, Mary, afterwards Countess of Buckingham. Created Baron Villiers and Earl of Anglesey 1623. Died 1630.   [c] William Herbert, Earl of Pembroke.

lique affayres, wherein, in my opinion, he dothe, as hathe ever bene esteemed, the part of a wise man.

The 13. of this monethe the Kinge in person satt in the Starre Chamber, about a duell intended to be performed betwene two gentlemen of the Innes of Court, the one called Christmas and the other Bellingham. In my last vnto you I wrote of them, but all was but a fallse rumor, beinge then geven out thatt they were bothe slayne in duell beyonde the seas, where they should have fought, but did not meete. After there cominge into England the quarrel revived, and by agreement they should have fought neere vnto Romeford, in Essex, where they were prevented by some meanes which the Lord Chiefe Justice of the Kinges Benche made, and this day (*ore tenus*) they were brought to the Starre Chamber. The Lords of the Counsayle onelye delivered there opinions and the Kinge himsellfe pronounced there censures, which was that ether of them should be imprisoned in the Tower duringe his Majesties pleasure, fined in one thousand pound the peece, to make there humble submissions in open court when itt should be required, nott to weare any weapon for the space of seven yeres, and at no tyme to come within tenne myles of the courts of his Majestie, of her Majestie, or of the Prince.

French princes proclaimed traitors.
In France the Dukes of Nevers, Vendosme, Mayne, Bovillon, and others, and allso the Marques of Coevre are proclaymed traytors, and the Kinge hathe an armye on foote, of 25,000 horse and foote, marchinge toward Champagne, and of this great armye the Duke of Gvise is the generall.

Death of Sir George Cary.
My olld shakinge kinsman, Sir George Cary,[a] sometymes Lord Deputie of Irland, is dead, and his wife is now a riche widdow.

The war in Italy.
In Piemont there hathe beene latelye an encountre vppon the borders of Millan; the comander of the Duke's forces was his eldest

---

[a] Sir George Cary, of Cockington, co. Devon. He was the grandson of Jane, daughter of Sir Nicholas, Baron Carew, of whom the Lord Carew was the direct lineal representative. Sir George Cary was twice married, but left no surviving issue. His widow was Lucy, daughter of Robert Lord Rich and Earl of Warwick.

sonne, the Prince Don Vittoria,[a] and with him his brother Don Tomaso.[b]   The Spanishe troopes were comanded by Don Sancho de Luna, the Chastelayne of the cittadell att Milan: the yonge princes charged them with suche furye as the Spaniards were rowted, and there commander, Don Sancho, lefte dead in the place, with losse of many of his men.

Vppon the necke of this newes other advertisements of good assurance was brought to the Kinge thatt the Duke of Savoy in Monferratt beseedged a towne called Saint Amien, a stronge place, well manned, munitioned, and victualled, neverthelesse the cannon made a fayre saultable breache; the defendants, fearinge the furye of an assault, demanded parlé, and in the end submitted themsellves to the law of the conqueror, who gave them there lives onlye, and so without bagage they departed; the spoyle of the towne was geven to the souldiours, and when there harpie hands had made an emptie towne, the Duke demolished the same, and vtterly defaced the wall, even to the foundation.   Frome thence with his victorious armye he marched to Alba, allso in Monferratt, and is now att the siedge thereof: the Duke's armye in the fild is 22,000 foote and 3,000 horse.

The Archdukes, by commandment out of Spayne, hathe sent towards Italye 6,000 foote and 1,000 horse, comanded by Don Gvillierro de Vendago, but how they will comme safelye thether tyme will discover.

Now att the last the Count John of Nassau is gone with his regiment for the ayde of the Venetians; he was stayed after his men was

---

[a] Victor Amadeus, eldest surviving son of Charles Emanuel Duke of Savoy, whom he succeeded as Duke of Savoy, and King of Cyprus, 1630.   He was a great lover of peace, but, being in 1635 drawn into a war between France and Spain, and overwhelmed with new cares, he was seized with a fever, of which in a few days he died, on 7th October, 1637.   He was born 1587, and in 1619 married Christina, daughter of Henry IV. King of France.—Andérson.

[b] Thomas Francis, Prince of Carignan, sixth son of Charles Emanuel, Duke of Savoy, born 1596.   He spent most of his life in the camp, and became an able though unfortunate general.   He served both Spain and France alternately, and, being wounded at the siege of Papua, he died at Turin, 22 January, 1656.—Anderson.

abord above 4 monethes for want of a wynde, and so did all the shippinge bound to the southward. Att the same tyme 9 great shipps for the East Indies departed from Holland.

Religious dis-
sensions in
Holland.

In the Vnited Provinces there is a mighty distraction about the matter of religion, somme enclininge to the opinion of Gomarus ᵃ and others hold with Arminius; this difference produceth yll effects, and is growne to such a beate as in the townes of Brill and Amsterdam the inhabitants have bene readie to fall to armes amonge themselves, and so itt is in other places. Yf the common enemye vnto them all (I mean the Spaniard) do not move to geve them cause to attend there generall defence, it is to be feared thatt a generall distraction will dissolve there vnion.

New bishops.

The Bishoppe of Bristow, Doctor Thorneboroghe,ᵇ is nowe Bishoppe of Worcester, and Doctor Feltonᶜ Byshoppe of Bristow.

French news.

In Paris a Scottyshe gentleman, called Steward, was executed for indeavouringe to levye men, and to send them to Soyssons in the

---

ᵃ Francis Gomar, born at Bruges, 1568. He was educated in England, and in 1594 became Professor of Divinity at Leyden. He was a zealous supporter of Calvinistic doctrines, and when Arminius was chosen his colleague in 1603, a difference arose between them on the subject of grace and predestination. Gomar conducted himself in the controversy with great violence, which led to the religious dissensions which prevailed in Holland for many years. He died 1641.

ᵇ Dr. John Thornborough, of Magdalene College, Oxford, Prebendary and Dean of York 1589, Bishop of Limerick 1593, Bristol 1603, Worcester 1616. Died 1641. " Doctor Thornborough is made Bishop of Worcester to make roome for Dr. Goodwin to be Deane of Yorke (though I heare he refuse yt), and Dr. Maxie to be Bishop of Bristow, that so your Archbishop of Spalato may (with a coadjutor) be Dean of Windsor. He is well esteemed and respected every where, specially at Court. On New Year's Day the King sent him a fayre basen and eure, with a paire of liverie pots, worth 140 *li.*, whereof he is not a little prowde. Dr. Montague is Dean of Hereford, and Dr. Lawde of Worcester, as I take yt. One Beaumont, an obscure prebend of Windsor, kinsman to my Lord Villiers, was in a fair way to be Bishop of Worcester, but the conferring of Carlisle and Bangor vpon Snowdon and Baylie, so vnworthie men, was so generally distasted that he could not prevaile."—Chamberlain to Carleton, 4 January, 1617. S. P. O. Dom. Corr. vol. xc. 8.

ᶜ Dr. Nicholas Fenton, one of the King's chaplains, attended Elwes at his execution, Prebendary of St. Paul's, Bishop of Bristol 1617, Ely 1619. Died 1628.

ayde of·the Duke de Mayne. Not farre frome Soyssons certayne
of the Kinges troopes, stragglinge throughe the countrye, were
charged ether by the Duke de Mayne or some of his, and the
number of 100 or thereabouts were slayne: they appertayned vnto
the Count of Candale, who, with the Duke of Rohan and divers
others of the religion, are in the Kinges armye; for in this discontentment of the princes the bodye of the religion dothe not move.
This is the first blood drawne thatt we have heard of since the late
troubles beganne.

This 26. of Februarye the Kinge of France in person beggane his
marche towards Rheims in Champagne.

✠ The Duke of Saxe [a] sollicitts continuallye the Emperor for the Dukedom of Jvlliers, wherein he pretends to have a right; the Pro-testant princes perswade him to desist, and to conioyne with them in there vnion. News from the Hague.

The Count Jean Jacomo Belgiese is raysinge in the country of
Liege 2 regiments of foote for the Kinge of France; and the Barons
of Recheme [b] and Anholt [c] are allso levienge 1000 horse for the
sayed Kinge.

The Marques Spinola, as itt is thought, will shortlye geve an
attempt to recover the Duchie of Bovillon frome the Duke, for the
which he is makinge great preparations

The Duke of Luneburge [d] earnestly sollicitts the Dukes of Saxe

---

[a] John George, 11th Duke of Saxony, 1611—56. He claimed the dukedom by virtue
of the purchase by his ancestor of the reversion of William III. Duke of Juliers, in 1483,
but upon the death of William his heiress carried all his possessions to the House of Cleve
and Marck, by her marriage with John III. Duke of Cleve.—Anderson.

[b] Herman de Lynden, imperial free Baron of Rechem and of Richolt, Governor and
Captain-General of the district of Cologne, Souverain and Grand Mayor of Liege.—
Anselme.

[c] Jean Jacques·de Bronchorst, Count of Anholt, Baron of Battembourg de Milendonck,
Master-General of the camp of the armies of the Emperor, Knight of the Golden Fleece
and of Mary Cleophas of Hollenzollern. Died 1630.—Anselme; Moreri.

[d] See note [b], p. 81.

CAMD. SOC.   N

and Mekellburge [a] and the Elector of Collen [b] to put him in possession of Grobenhagen, as by the decree of the Imperiall Chamber they
were authorised.   On the contrarye part, the Duke of Brunswicke
will not submitt himsellfe vnto the sentence, and prepares for his
defence.

The two French regiments which serve the Estates are sent for by
the Frenche Kinge to serve him agaynst the princes, but itt is
thought thatt nether the Estatts will lett them to depart, or that they
are willinge to leave there service.

The Emperour bathe published an edict throughout all Germanye,
to inhibit any munition or vtensilles for the warre to be sent into
France vnto the Princes partie, and allso the levies of men is inhi-
bited; but it is thought thatt the edict will not be obeyed.

The Duke of Savoy, as is sayed, entends to enter with his forces
into the Duchye of Millan; the princes in France are muche incou-
raged by his prosperous successes, and his ambassadors are daylye
expected in the Low Countries to treat with the Estates to ioyne in a
strict league with him.

The Kinge of Denmarke hathe 24 shipps in a readiness to put to
the sea, as itt is thought in the ayde of the Kinge of Sweden agaynst
the Kinge of Poland, who intends to make warre vppon Sweden.

The Counte of Levesteyne,[c] who hathe levied 3,000 men in
Germanye for the succour of the Venetians, hathe sent two captons
and the lettres of the Republique of Venice vnto the Estates
gencrall, to permitt them passage through there territories, and to
permitt them to hyre shippinge (for there money) to transport

---

[a] Adòlph Frederic I. Patriarch of the line of Schwerin, or the Lutheran line, born
1588, succeeded 1592; but, for siding with Christian IV. of Denmark, he, with his brother,
were proscribed, and his duchy given to Albert Wallensteine, Duke of Friedland, 1628,
but he was again restored to it by Gustavus Adolphus, 1631.   Died 1658.

[b] Ferdinand, Elector 1612—50, born 1577.   Bishop of Liege, Munster, and Hilde-
sheim 1612, and of Paderborn 1619.   Died 1650.—Anderson.

[c] Christopher Lewis, Count of Loewenstein, the Patriarch of the Virneburg or
Lutheran line, born 1568.   Died 1618.—Anderson.

theme by longe seas vnto Venice. From this ✠ hetherto is the
newes from the Hage.

The 27. of this monethe Sir Edward Cecill was maried to Diana General newes.
Drewrye, sister to the Ladye Burghlie, and coheyre vnto Sir Robert
Drewrye.[a]

Marche.—The first of this monethe your olld frend and myne Sir March.
Edward Hobye[b] died att his house att Bisham, in Barkshire, and
hathe lefte his bastard sonne his heyre, nott so much as once remem-
beringe his brother Sir Thomas Hobye with any thinge which he
could take from him.

Sir Allen Apsley,[c] the 3. of this monethe, was sworne lieutenant
of the Tower in the roome of Sir George Moore, who was wearye of
thatt troublesome and dangerous office.

The Queene vppon Shrovetwesday made the Kinge a great feast
at Queenes Court, sometyme Somersett House, and now agayne re-
baptised and called Denmarke House.

The Lord Evre[d] (vppon good consideration) hathe rendered the
Precidencye of Wales vnto the Lord Gerrard,[e] who is now Lord
President.

Before the departure of Monsieur de la Tour, the Frenche Kinges
Extraordinarye Ambassador, the Lord Hay feasted him att the
Wardrobe,[f] which, in a word, was the most magnificent feast thatt

---

[a] See note ε, p. 4.

[b] Sir Edward Hoby, of Bisham Abbey, co. Berks, knighted 1582. Gentleman of the
Privy Chamber to Queen Elizabeth, and Governor of Queenborough Castle.

[c] Sir Allen Apsley. His wife, a daughter of Sir John St.John, of Lydiard Tregoze,
was a sister of Sir Edward Villiers' lady. Sir Allen paid Sir George Moore a composition
of £2,500 for the place.—Birch, i. 462. He was the father of Lucy Hutchinson, wife of
the celebrated Colonel Hutchinson, in whose life some interesting particulars of Sir
Allen may be found.

[d] Ralph third Lord Eure, made President of Wales 1607. He died in April of this
year; see p. 99.

[e] Gilbert second Lord Gerard.

[f] Chamberlain says that this feast stood the Lord Hay "in more than £2,200, being rather
a profusion and spoil than reasonable or honourable provision, as you may guess at the rest

ever I have seene in my life without exception; and after supper a
maske equall to those which you have seene att Whitehall, whereatt
most of the Englishe and Scottishe Lords and great ladies then in
town were present: itt was about the last of Februarye.

There is att Gibraltarr a great fleete of Spayne assembled, composed of the whole armada royall, the West India fleet thatt brought
home the last treasure into Spayne, and of nine great shipps buillt,
as was geven out, to goe for the Phillipines: they have in them
32,000 land souldiours, and the Duke of Savoy's second sonne is
the generall.[a]   The galleys of Naples, Scicilie, Ligorne, Malta, Barcelona, and of other ports, meete and ioyne with the fleet at
Maiorque.   They have allso 200 tartenas, which are a kind of
flat-bottomde boates which draw nott above 2 or 3 foot of water, to
land men, also they have a provision of 400 great masts, 1,500 three-
yuche planke to land ordnance or to make platformes on the water.

They are likewise provided with 6,000 musketts, and armes for
20,000 men, att least, more then they have use of, to arme there
frends where they go, but whether itt is no man knowes but those
which are of thatt counsayle: from the Archduke 20 pilotts was
sent vuto them; every one of them was imprested with 100 ducatts,
and 50 ducatts to every of there wives.

They embarge all nations, enforcinge them to serve in the expedition, Frenche onely excepted.   There is an edict published,
comandinge all men to forbeare tradinge vnto Brasill in caravells,

by this scantling—of seven score pheasants, twelve partridges in a dish throughout, twelve
whole salmons, and whatsoever else that cost or curiosity could procure in like superfluity,
besides the workmanship and invention of thirty cooks for twelve days." "But," he continues,
"the ill luck was, that the chief and most desired guest was away; for the young Lady
Sidney, with her sister, the Lady Lucy Percy, going, sbme two or three days before the
feast, to visit their father in the Tower, after some few caresses he dismissed his daughter
Sidney to go to her husband, and to send her sister's maids to attend her, for that he meant
not to part with her, but she should keep him company ; adding withal, that he was a
Percy, and could not endure that his daughter should dance any Scottish *jig*."—Birch, i.
462. The old Earl's caution was however of no avail. She was married to the Lord
Hay in November following against her father's will.

[a] Don Tomaso; see note [b], p. 87.

for they were the pray of the piratts, and not to traffique thether but in shippes which could carrye att the least 14 peeces of ordinance. This report was brought into England by an English Mr., who protested thatt he was an eye witnesse of this preparation. Vppon what land this storme will fall we shall shortlye know.

The 5. of this monethe the great seal of England was taken frome the Lord Chanceler,[a] nott for any cryme or conceyved displeasure against him, but because of his dangerous sicknes, whereby he is‑ growne weake and vnable to exercise his office; accompanied with his owne request vnto the Kinge, who came to visite him. *English news.*

The 7. the seale was delivered to Sir Francis Bacon, and the same day he was at the counsell table sworne Lord Keeper of the great seale. The olld Chanceler, as itt is conceved, will deale no more in publique affayres, but attend his quiett.

Sir Henry Yelverton [b] is now his Majesties Attorney-Generall, and Mr. Coventrye, the Recorder of London, his Majesties Solliciter, and Mr. Ben,[c] of the Middle Temple, Recorder of London.

The Kinge of Sweden hathe concluded a peace with the Muscovite, and his ambassadors were in the Vnited Provinces to gett leave to levye men there against the Kinge of Poland. *Foreign news.*

The Lorde of Salinas in Spayne is latelye created Marques Alanquer, and is to go viceroy into Portugall.[d]

The Cardinall of Toledo[e] is thought to be so dangerouslye sicke as thatt he cannott recover; and a nephew vnto the Duke of Lerma, sonne to his sister the Countesse de Altamira, is like to be his successor.

a Sir Thomas Egerton, Lord Viscount Braekley.

b Sir Henry Yelverton, son of Sir Christopher Yelverton, Judge of the King's Bench. Knighted in 1613, on his appointment as Solicitor-General. Died 1630.

c Sir Antony Benn, of Norbeton Hall, near Kingston-upon-Thames, of which place he had been Recorder. Knighted 1617. Died 1618. His daughter Annabella married Henry Earl of Kent, and from her benevolent disposition was called the " good countess."

d See note b, page 83.

e Bernard de Sandoval de Roxas, Grand Inquisitor, and Archbishop of Toledo, created Cardinal 1598. Died 1618, and was succeeded by François Roxas Sandoval, who died 1625.

A shippe of Leethe, in Scotland, of the burden of 200 tunnes, is taken by the Turkishe pirattes within the Straytes, and in her Sir William Carre, a Scottishe gentleman, and others, were slayne, and the rest with the shippe carried to Angire.

The Archduke Ferdinand, of Gratz, makes all the vnderhand meanes he may to be Emperour after Mathias.

The Archdukes in the Low Countries favour, in all they may, the Kinge, and do whatt in them lyes to empeach the Princes of France.

The Duke of Espernon beinge [sent] for by the queene-mother to come to the Kinge, vsed Monsieur de Zamett, who was the messenger, with all the humanitie he could, but made his excuses, and would not move.

The Mareschall d'Ancre raysed 5,000 foote in Lakeland and the countries thereabouts; 2,000 of them embarqued att Dunkerke, and landed att Fescampe in Normandie; the other 3000 are likewise to be shipped there, and so brought vnto him.

The distraction about religion in the Vnited Provinces encreasethe. Barnevevallt [a] is a great vpholder of the Arminians, and, as men suppose, a papist; he is a favourer of the French Kinges cause agaynst the Princes.

The Duke of Vendosme and his vncle, the Marquis de Coevre, do now profess themselves to be Protestants,* as de Molines, the preacher, hathe advertised his Majestie, which lettres came the 10. of this monethe.

The town of Alba, in Monferrat, is rendered to the Duke of Savoy, which the Duke delivered vnto Monsieur Le Mareschall de Digueres.

The Duke of Mantua [b] hathe latelye maried the Duke of Florence his second sister.

---

* Suspend your judgement.

---

[a] John d'Olden Barneveldt, executed 1619.

[b] Ferdinand, born 1587, created Cardinal 1605, succeeded his brother as Duke of Mantua and Montferrat 1612. Dièd 1626. He first married Camilla Retecina, from whom he was divorced 1616, when he married, as stated in the text, Catherine, daughter of Ferdinand Grand Duke of Florence.

The States of the Vnited Provinces have the towne of Sedan into there protection, with promise to ayde the same (yff itt be attempted) att all tymes.   •

There is now in France 3 armies in the feld, one commanded by the Duke of Gvise, in Champagne, another by the Count d'Avvergne, necre vuto Paris, and the third vnder the command of the Marshall D'Ancre, in Normandie.

The Duke of Rohan is the generall of horse vnder the Counte d'Avvergne.

Mr. Henry Bartie,[a] the yongest brother to the Lord Willoghby, is now att Rome, prisoner in the Inquisition; how he will be able to free himsellfe out of the Inquisitors divelishe clawes is to be feared.

This 14. Marche the Kinges Majestie beginnes his jorney towards The King's Scotland; his first remove is Theobalds; the quene, the prince, and journey to all his counsayle, attends him; and from thence with his selected Scotland. trayne he departs.   God send him a prosperous and short retourne!

Latelye in thatt kingdome a difference hathe fallen out betwene the Marques Huntley[b] and the Erle of Arrell,[c] which by partiallities were like to put a flame in itt, for they are on ether side strong in freuds and followers, but the Kinges presence amongst them (I hope in God) will make a pacification, otherwise itt is conceved thatt muche mischiefe would ensue.

Of men of quallitie there attends his Majestie into Scotland—

The Duke of Lennox, Lord Steward,

The Erle of Pembroke, Lord Chamberlayne,

The Erle of Arundell,

The Erle of Rutland,

The Erle of Southampton,

The Erle of Montgomerye,

The Erle of Buckingham, Master of the Horse,

[a] Henry Bertie, third son of Peregrine Bertie, first Baron Willoughby d'Eresby of his name.   Died 1655.

[b] George Gordon, first Marquis of Huntly.

[c] Francis Hay, eighth Earl of Errol.

The Lord Dowbenye,[a]

The Viscount Fenton, Capten of the Gvard,

The Vicecount Haddington,   •

The Lord Walden,[b] Capten of the Pentioners,

The Lord Mordant,[c]

The Lord Compton,[d]

The Lord Hay, Master of the Gvardrobe,

Mr. Secretary Lake,

The Bishoppe of Winchester,[e] Deane of Chapple,

The Bishoppe of Elye,[f] Almosiner,

The Bishoppe of Lincolne,[g] clarke of the closet; besides many northern noblemen thatt meet him vppon the way in Yorkshire. There is allso many gentlemen of marque, noblemen's sones, knights, &c., which is to longe to relate.

The Lord Chanceler died the 15. day of this monethe att Yorke house, leavinge to his posteritie an huge estate.

General news. The Duke of Saxe is entred into the vnion with the Protestant Princes in Germanye, and the Duke of Savoy hathe subscribed to the same.

In Germanye there is great levies of men, as well for the Kinge of France as for the Princes proscribed.

The Duchesse of Brunswicke (her Majesties fathers sister) is latelye dead.

Sir John Egerton, Viscount Brackley, sonne to the late Lord

---

[a] Esme Stuart, Lord d'Aubigny, created Earl of March 1619. Succeeded his brother as third Duke of Lennox 1624, and died the same year.

[b] Theophilus Howard, eldest son of the Earl of Suffolk, called to the Upper House as Lord Howard of Walden (1603) in his father's lifetime. Earl of Suffolk 1626. Died 1640.

[c] John fifth Lord Mordaunt, created Earl of Peterborough 1628. Died 1642.

[d] William Compton, second Baron Compton, created Earl of Northampton on the 2nd of August in this year, K.G. Died 1630.

[e] Dr. James Mountague.

[f] Dr. Andrewes.   [g] Dr. George Mountaine.

Chanceler, is created by lettres patents Earl of Bridgewater, but they are nott yett delivered vnto him.

Sir Edward Nowel [a] is created a Baron of Parliament.

The Lord Hay is sworne a counceler.

The Lord Rosse the 21. of this monethe came to London, from whence he must follow the Kinge, to geve an accompt of his negotiation in Spayne.

The Lord Audeley, who latelye in Irland was created Erle of Castelhaven and Baron Orier,[b] is newlye dead.

It is sayed that the Duke of Florence, in ayde of his brother-in- *Foreign news.* law the Duke of Mantua, sends vnto him 14,000 foote and 2,000 horse. There passage throughe the territorie of Modena is denied, for (as we know) thatt duke's sonne hathe maried a daughter of Savoy. Itt is threatened thatt they will force there way,—but the truthe of the forces above mentioned *vix credo.* Don Giovanni de Medicis, bastard brother to the Duke Florence's father, is the generall of the Venetian's land armye agaynst the Archduke Ferdinand, commonlye called the Duke of Gratz, or ells the gazette from Venice is fallse.

The great armado of Spayne with the land armye in itt is dissolved, whether itt was to go, or what the cause of the dissolution, is not yett so vulgar as thatt I cane geve you an accompt of itt: itt is sayed itt brake for want of victualls.

This 28. Marche Sir Wallter Raleghe's shippe fell downe the river *Raleghes* vuto the Downes, and himselfe is gone overland to Dover. Vntill he *expedition.* come to Plimouthe (where is the rendevous of his little fleet) I cannott exactlye send you a report either of his shippes, captens, or men. He goes for the Orenoquen myne. God graunt he may retourne deepe loden with Gvianian gold oure!

The Holland fleet is retourned frome the East Indies. Of the Hollanders' actions in those parts, and particularlye att Malacca, I forbeare to write, beinge better knowne vnto you then vnto us.

Sir Edward Noel, created Lord Noel of Ridlington, co. Rutland.

[b] See note [c], p. 44.

Sir John Digbye, the King's Vicechamberlayne, is to be dis-patched Ambassador into Spayne; Sir ·Thomas Edmonds, his Majesties Comptroller, to be dispatched Ambassador into France; and Sir John Bennet,[a] her Majesties Chancellor, is sent Ambassador to the Archdukes: but none of them make any longe stay in those employments.

Some four or five of your men, lefte in the River of Amazons, are richelye retourned in a Holland shippe; the rest of your men re-mayne there, those which are come home are ryche, and (as I heare) they meane to retourne: itt is sayed, that these five brought with them so much tobacco, as they have sold in the Low Countries, where they first arrived, and in England, for 2,300[li].; and allso itt is reported thatt they brought some ingotts of gold, butt to whatt valew I know nott.

Foreign news. The Duke of Espernon keepes in the cittie of Bordeaux. He is nether for the King nor for the Princes; but in this sturringe world he is nott ydle, for he drawes men vnto him, and for there payment he is bold of the Kinges revenew in those parts, takinge uppe to his own vse as muche as he cane lay hands vppon.

Those of the religion do nott yett move, but to prevent dangers (which may fall out to there preiudice) they have agreed vppon an assemblye att Rochell: the Kinge forbids itt, but yett they go on, and Rochell allso beinge required to the contrarye, yett they will hazard all rather then refuse there olld frends.

The Duke of Ossuna,[b] Viceroy of Naples, threatens the Venetians to visite them shortlye with a fleete in the Gullphe of Venice; the State provides for his comminge: the salutations betwene theme

---

[a] Sir John Bennet, of Dawley, co. Middlesex, D.C.L., a man of great learning and ability, knighted 1603. He was frequently employed in important matters of state. The object of the present mission was to demand from the Archduke an explanation concern-ing a libel published, as was supposed, by Erycius Puteanus, which the Archduke took no care to suppress or to punish the author. Sir John was the ancestor of the Tankerville family. Died 1627.

[b] Peter Giron, second Duke of Ossuna, born 1579. Died 1624.

will be cannon language; some are of opinion that the late dissolved Spanishe armada was for Venice. The difference betwene
thatt state and Spayne arisethe from the warre which longe since
hathe bene on foote betwene the Archduke of Gratz and theme.

Aprill.—In my laste I wrote vuto you, that there was a wicked Apr l.
Home news.
villanous booke written agaynst the Kinge, and itt was supposed to
be Barkley's writinge,[a] but now the truthe appeares thatt it was
written by one Puteanus, a lecturer in the Vniversitye att Lovayne:
Sir John Bennett amonge other matters hathe instructions to deale
with the Archduke about him, to be made an example for scandaliz-
inge annoynted Kinges.

The Lord Evre is dead.[b]

The Lord of Hunsdon [c] is dead.

Mr. Thomas Warre, a Counceler-att-law, who I thinke was well
knowne vnto you, is latelye drowned in Severn in Walles.

Sir Charles Candishe,[d] the Countess of Shrewsburies brother, is
dead.

France is now in every part in a flame: latelye the noblesse of French news.
Gvyenne wrote unto the Kinge a remonstrance of there aggreave-
ances, wherein they complayned principallye vppon the Marshall de
Ancre, and how insupportable his arrogancye and greatnes is to be
endured, and thatt vntill remedie were taken for quietinge of France
they professed to be bolld with the Kinges revenews and when he
came to riper yeres they would make him an accompt how they had
disposed of itt. In these partes all the protestants and catholiques
ioyne in this resolution. The men of greatest note thatt are in

---

[a] See p. 37.

[b] Ralph, third Lord Eure. Nicolas states that he was alive in 1623, but he died on the
1st April, 1617.—Pedigree in Coll. Arm. Norfolk ix.

[c] John Cary, third Lord.

[d] Sir Charles Cavendish of Bothal Castle, near Morpeth, younger brother of the first
Earl of Devonshire, knighted 1603.

armes in those parts are the Dukes of Memorency, Trimoville,[a] and Espernon.

Betwene the Princes confederate in the parts of Picardie and Champagne and the Kinges armies comanded by the Duke of Gvise and the Count de Avvergne skirmishes passe, and men slayne on ether side, and pettie places are taken, but as yett no greatt blow hathe beene geven on ether part.

The Princes Confederatts have nott yett put into the fild; every one stayes within his owne precinct, as the Duke of Vesdosme att La Fere, the Duke of Nevers att Masieres, the Duke de Mayne att Soyssons, the Duke of Bvillon att Sedan, and so the rest, nether yett do we heare of any great towne put into there hands.

In Germanye great levies of horse and foote are made on ether part, and strangers on all sides are on there way to pillage France.

It is sayed thatt the Emperour will this sommer come into Cleve with an army to possess himsellfe of those Duchies vntill the right be decided, which moves both the States of the Vnited Provinces, and the Confederatt Princes protestants in Germanye, to rayse forces to prevent a storme which may fall vppon theme.

The Kinge of Sweden rayses men in the Low Countries to resist the Kinge of Poland's invasion vppon him.

The Kinge of Denmarkes fleet, whereof I have heretofore sayed somewhatt,[*][b] moves bothe the Vnited Provinces and the Hanse townes to arme to the sea, and betwene them a greatt fleet is prepared to resist the Kinge of Denmarke desseygne, butt whatt thatt is is nott yett knowne.

The supplies sent frome the Vnited Provinces vnder the conduct of the Count John of Nassau are safelye passed the Strayghts of

---

[*] All this preparation proved no other than a voyage the King made to the northerly parts of Norway.

Henry de la Tremouille, Duke of Thouars, Peer of France, Prince of Tarentum and of Talmond, Comte de Laval. He abjured the doctrines of Calvin 1628. Died 1674.

[b] See p. 90.

Gibraltar, and, vndoubtedlye, they be arrived att Venice; the Kinge of Spaynes dissolved fleet beinge then att Cadiz.

The difference betwene the Dukes of Brunswicke and Lvneburge is determined, and the Duchie of Grobenhagen (for which they contended) is put into the Duke of Luneburg's possession.

The ayde from Holland sent to the Venetians is safelye arrived att Venice, whereat muche ioy was made.

The Duke of Ossuna intends to visite the Gullphe of Venice with a fleet frome Naples: to welcome him thether the States have armed to the sea 30 gallies, 4 gallyasses, 5 Dutche shippes, and some others.

The Kinge of France, wearye, as itt appeares, to be helld by the Queene his mother as a minore, and allso grieved to see the calamitie of France daylie encreasinge, takinge spiritt vnto him, and by advice of somme of his trustie servants in whose faythe he was confident, concluded thatt itt was necessarye for him to take the life of the Mareschall d'Ancre, beinge the readiest meanes for a pacification. The Mareschall, as he was accustomed, comeinge in the morninge to the Lovre, vppon the drawbridge, the 14th of Aprill, according to our style, Monsieur de Vitrie,[a] sonne to the old Vitrie, and one of the Captens of the Kinges ordinarie gardes, accompanied with some gentlemen and about twentie of the gard, mett with him and tolld him thatt by the Kinges comandment he did arrest him the Kinges prisoner; the Mareschall wondered att the summons, and was slow in obeyinge. Vitre givinge a signe to his companie they instantlye shott him throughe the head and body, and being dead in the place divers wounds were geven him with swords. Vitre enteringe into the court cried Vive le Roy; the Kinge beinge in his chamber window askt him whatt was done. Vitre tolld him he had slayne the Mareschall de Ancre; the Kinge approved the fact, and sent presentlye

Death of Marshal D'Ancre.

---

[a] Nicholas de l'Hôpital, Marquis of Vitry and Arc, Captain of the King's Body Guard, created Marshal of France 24 April 1617 (see p. 103), Knight of the Orders of the King 1619, Governor of Provence 1632, made Duke and Peer of France 1644, and died the same year. He was the son of Louis de l'Hôpital, Marquis of Vitry.

to the magistrats of the cittie and to the court of parliament decla-
ringe thatt for the good of France, which was distempered, thatt he
had caused the life of Ancre to be taken, avowinge itt to be his own
comandment.   He allso sent to the Bastille to his cosen the Prince
of Conde, willinge him to be of good cheere, for now all should be
well.   The Mareschall's wife, Madame de Ancre,[a] is in safe keep-
inge.   The Garde de Seaux monsieur Margott,[b] the bishoppe of
Luzon[c] the Secretarye, and Barbin the Comptroller of the Finances,
beinge three principall favorers of the Mareschall and placed in
there offices by him, are all restrayned and removed frome there
places.

The queene mother vppon the deathe of Ancre sent to the Kinge
to desire him to come vnto her, which he excused for as then he
had no leasure; and whereas formerlye she was ever accustomed to
have a gard of her owne to attend her, the Kinge bathe removed
them frome her and commanded a gard of his owne to supplie there
romes.   This great action vndowtedly is done without the privitie
of the Queene, or with the knowledge of any of the Spanishe
Councell; itt was meerlye the Kinges owne, to free himsellfe and the
realme frome danger, and certaynlye itt carries a fayre probabilitie
towards the pacification of France.

Vppon the notice of his deathe the Magistrats of the cittie of

___

[a] See note ᵍ, p. 26.   The Duke of Rohan, speaking of the Marshal d'Ancre just before
this time, says, "It were not to be desired that he should be ruined, for his birth is equal
to any that in our memory hath been created not only Marshal but Duke and Peer of
France, and his wit and education and many other qualities make him to be thought
worthy of this favour, and to be naturalized to perpetuate his family among us, which
would be a great honour to our nation."   He says, on the other hand, that it was without a precedent that a man should be honoured with the dignity of Marshal of France who
had never served in an army; or be at once entrusted with the seals and the purse of the
King : that is to say, with his whole authority; and that such power, vested in a single person, was dangerous to the state and monarchy.—Memoirs of the Duke of Rohan.

[b] See note ᵈ, p. 42.

[c] Armand Jean du Plessis Richelieu, afterwards the celebrated Cardinal Richelieu.
He was consecrated Bishop of Luçon 1608, created Cardinal 1622, and resigned his
bishopric on being made the King's chief minister 1624.   Died 1642.

Paris, the Court of Parliment, those of the Religion which were in
the towne, and all sorts of men, repayred to the Kinge, applaudinge
and magnifyinge the act.   His bodie was by the people taken out of
the ground, hanged vppe by the heeles on a gibbett, torne and cutt in
peeces with as muche opprobrie and scorne as could be vsed to a
dead carcase, and lastly, by peecemeale, burned to ashes in divers
parts of the towne.

Madame de Ancre is now committed prisoner to the Bastill, and
so is Margott, the gard seaux.

Barbin the Comptroller of the finnances is allso a prisoner, and his
triall, iudicially, is expected.

Monsieur de Vair, who was the garde de seaux [a] (when Sillerye
was displaced from the execution of the office of chanceler), is agayne
restored; Monsieur de Villeroy,[b] who had geven over his place of
secretarye, is recalled; Monsieur de Sillerye,[c] and his sonne Monsieur
de Puisseaux, one of the secretaries, are now agayne in grace and
favour; Monsieur de Vitre is made a marshall of France; his brother,
Monsieur de Halliar,[d] is, in his place, one of the captens of the garde,
and Monsieur de Pressan,[e] who married his sister (who with de
Halliar were with Vitre when the Mareschall de Ancre was slayne),
is the capten of the Bastill; Monsieur de Lvines,[f] a gentleman born

See note [d] p. 42.

[b] Nicholas de Neufville, Seigneur of Villeroy, died 12 Nov. 1617.

[c] Nicholas Brulart, Marquis of Sillery and Seigneur of Puisseaux.   Died at an advanced age 1624.   It was this nobleman who was sent into Spain in 1615, as recorded in
page 3, and not his son, as erroneously stated in the note to that passage.   The latter,
during his father's life, appears to have been called Monsieur de Puisseaux. He died in
1640.—Anselme.

[d] François de l'Hôpital, Comte de Rosnay, Seigneur du Hallier, and of Beine, Governor
of Paris, created Marshal of France 1643.   Died 1660.—Anselme.

[e] Henry de Vandetar, Baron of Persan, married Louise de l'Hôpital, daughter of Louis
de l'Hôpital, Marquis of Vitry.—Anselme.

[f] Charles d'Albert, born 1578, Seigneur de Luynes, Grand Falconer, created Duke of
Luynes 1619, and in 1621 Constable of France.   He married 1617, Marie, eldest daughter
of Hercules de Rohan, Duke of Montbazon.—Anselme.   Died of grief at the failure
before Montauban 1621.—Yonge's Diary, p. 48.

about Avignon, who is very inward with the Kinge, and supposd
to be the principall adviser of the Mareschall de Ancre his deathe,
succeeds him in the Kinges chamber, beinge now (as he was) le
premier gentlehome du chambre du Roy, and allso his successor in
the lieutenancye of Normandie. The queene mother is in some sorte
restrayned of her libertie, and attended by speciall gardes, and itt is
thought she shall be confined to Amboyse or Molins in Bourbonnois.
The Kinge recalls his armies. He sent of late money to the Duke de
Mayne (who was at Ancre his deathe beseedged att Soyssons), to
pay his troopes to dismisse them, and the like will be done (as it is
thought) with the other Princes, and a generall peace in France
expected.

The government of Caen in Normandie is geven to the Chevalier
de Vendosme, the Kinges base brother, and allso the abbey of
Normoustier, which the Mareschall de Ancre's brother had.

Marriage of Sir William Seymour.   About 3 monethes past Sir William Seymer,[a] the Erle of Hertford's grandchild, and husband to the Ladye Arabella, was married
to one of the Erle of Essex daughters: his grandfather assures vuto
him above 3,000ˡⁱ. by the yere of good inheritance.

May. French news.   *May.*—After the deathe of the Mareschall d'Ancre the King
never spake with the queene his mother untill she was in her
coach readie to depart out of Paris to go vuto the castle att Blois,
where she is assigned to live. At the instant of her departure
(to satisfie her desire) the Kinge came unto her, but his pleasure
was first signified how farre and in whatt sorte her speeche
should tend, and thatt she should nott speake but within those
limits. The substance of her speeche was, thatt she was sorry
thatt she could do him no further service in the affayres of estate,
prayinge him to beleeve thatt she had employed her best care and

---

[a] Succeeded his grandfather as Earl of Hertford 1621. Created Duke of Somerset
1660. Died the same year. He married Frances, eldest daughter of Robert second Earl
of Essex, and sister and coheir of Robert third Earl. She died 1674.

zeale therein, and thatt she would nott have spared her life for the advancement of his good; thatt she would allwayes acknowledge him to be her Kinge, and she hoped allso thatt he would nott forgett her to be his mother, and (with reiteration) his good mother. She prayed God to assist him with good counsayles in his affayres, and interceded somewhatt for Barbin the Comptroller of the Fynances. The Kinge gave many thankes for her care and paynes, and assured her thatt he would be ever readie to geve her contentment in all thatt was in his power.

Then she complemented a little while with Monsieur de Lvynes, gevinge him assurance of her good affection vnto him.

Betwene her and the yonge Queene the takinge of leave seemed to be somewhat confused, as yf the Queene mother had some touche of envye att the honnours she was to leave.

In passinge through the towne of Paris there appeared in her countenance rather menacinge then deiection.

She was accompanied with the two princesses her daughters, a great troope of ladies, her owne guarde, and a cornett of 50 horse, comanded by Monsieur de Curre.

As soon as the Mareschall d'Ancre was slayne the Kinge wrote Peace in vnto the Dukes of Vendosme, Nevers, Mayenne, and the Marques France. Coevre; vppon the receypt whereof, within a few dayes, they came vnto him, the day after his mother's departure, and found him with the Queene att Bois de Vincennes, where they were graciouslye receved, and they made there submissions.[a]

The Duke of Bvillon came nott with them, for he had received no lettres from the Kinge; yett he wrote his humble submission, and therevppon the Kinge hathe sent vnto him, and his cominge to Paris is expected.

Certayne troopes of horse levied in Germanye were vppon there way as farre as the Bishoppe of Triers territorie, the Duke of Bvillon

---

[a] The Duke of Rohan says: " Every one returns to Court, where all strive who should soonest and most impudently renounce that which but four-and twenty hours before they adored."—Memoirs of the Duke of Rohan, p. 42. (Lond. 1660.)

sent to staye them, but they without present pay will not stay there marche:* where vppon the Kinge hathe commanded the Duke of Gvise with his armye to draw to the frontiers, and yf they enter into Frenche ground to charge them as enemies; whatt will be the yssue a few dayes will discover.

The armies vnder the Count d'Avvergne and the Mareschall de Montignie, are, by the Kinges comandment, dissolved.

Frome those of the Religion tenne substitutes (whereof four frome Rochell) have beene sent to the Kinge, as well to congratulate the deathe of Ancre as to render hym thankes for the peace of France.

Barbin, the Comptroller of the Finances, is sent prisoner to the Bastill.

La Mareschalle d'Ancre is presentlye to be proceeded with for her life, for vntill she be convicted the Mareschall cannott be confiscated, for all his purchases and the substance of his great estate was passed vnder her name.

Of the prince of Conde's enlardgment as yet nothinge appeares.

General news. Sir Morice Barkeley [a] is latelye dead, who was a gentleman, as you know, of many good parts.

Your olld acquayntance Mr. Hackwell, the lawyer, is latelye maried to the yonge Ladye Killygrewes sister,[b] whereby he hathe gotten good frends in the Chancerie, for the Lord Keeper is her vncle, and the Master of the Rolles her brother-in-law, his last wife beinge another of Sir William Woodhouse his sisters.

The Duke of Longveville is maried to the olld Count Soyssons [c] daughter, and sister to the yonge Count Soyssons, who is about 14 yere olld.

---

* Since that tyme the King of France hathe sent 100,000 crownes to pay them.

---

[a] Sir Maurice Berkeley married Elizabeth, daughter of Sir William and sister of Sir Robert Killigrew of Hanworth, and resided there. He was the father of Sir John Berkeley, so much distinguished for his loyalty and services in the next reign, for which, in 1658, he was created Baron Berkeley of Stratton.

[b] Her mother was Bacon's sister, and her sister Sir Julius Cæsar's wife; see note [b], p. 11.

[c] Aloisa, daughter of Charles Count de Soissons and sister of Lewis. She was born 1604, and died 1637. See note [a], p. 46.

Sir John Denham, the Lord Chief Justice of Irland, is now latelye made one of the Barons of thexchequer in England. Sergeant Hvtton [a] is a judge in the roome of Justice Nicolls, Sir William Jones of Lincolns Iune [b] goes Lord Chief Justice into Irland, and Mr. Hackwell, your olld frend, is the Queen's sollicitor in the roome of Mr. Lowther,[c] who goes to be a judge into Irland.

In France, a priest named de Truvayte, of 50 yeres of age, French news. attempted the Baron of Brislew her grand esquire to murder the Queene, sayinge thatt itt was necessarie to accomplishe the worke in killinge her as well as the Marshall d'Ancre; and allso he perswaded Monsieur de Lvynes to the same, but nether of them would geve care vnto him. His practice was revealed; De Brissev and Lvynes chardged him, he could nott denye itt, and for his fowle intent he was broke vppon the wheele. The Marshall d'Ancre his wife is removed from the Bastill to the Conciergerie in Paris, a common gaole as our Newgate, and her triall is daylye expected. The Princes which were in armes are denounced to be faultlesse, and no offence is layed to there charge, for the Marshall d'Ancre his tyrannye enforced them to take armes for there necessarye defence, and now they are quitted.

Sir Thomas Edmonds is gone Embassador into France, and Sir General news. John Digbye is shortlye to go into Spayne.

The Bishoppe of Durham,[d] my olld schoolmaster, is dead, but a

[a] Sir Richard Hutton, second son of Anthony Hutton of Penrith, co. Cumberland. He was Recorder of York, where he was knighted by the King on 13th April in this year. His son, Sir Richard, supported the royal cause in the next reign, and was killed at the battle of Sherburne, in Yorkshire, of which he was then Sheriff.—Clarendon, ii. 717-718.

[b] Made Chief Justice of the King's Bench in Ireland 1617, returned to England as a puisne justice in 1621. See several notices of him in the Liber Famelicus of Sir James Whitelocke.

[c] Lancelot Lowther was Queen's Solicitor 1603, and made Baron of the Exchequer in Ireland Oct. 3, 1617, on the recommendation of Sir Francis Bacon. He died Jan. 10, 1637, and was buried at Skryne. co. Meath.

[d] Dr. William James, son of John James of Little Ore, co. Stafford, Dean of Durham 1596, Bishop 1606. Died 12 May, 1617.

few dayes after he had fayted the Kinge in his pallace: itt is thought thatt Doctor Neale,[a] the Bishoppe of Lincolne, shall succeed him.

The Kinge is now att Edinboroghe.

Sir Roger Owen,[b] the great parliment man, is distracted: itt may be feared thatt to muche learninge made him madde; and within a few dayes after he died.

The Erle of Buckingham is sworne a Counceller in Scottland.

The Kinge of Poland hathe assembled an armye to invade Sweden, betwene whom and the Muscovite a peace was latelye concluded, and they are confederated agaynste the Kinge of Pole, there common enemye.[c]

The Countesse of Salisburie is latelye delivered of a daughter.

The 26. of this monethe Sir Walter Raleghe was nott gone out of Plimouthe, enforced to remayne there for the comminge of some of his consorts vnto him, but his victualls spent he hathe supplied.

The faction in religion amonge the Netherlanders betwene the Gomarians and the Arminians encreasethe in great fervencie on ether part, which cannott but produce fearfull effects in the Vnited Provinces.

[a] Dr. Richard Neile, Clerk of the Closet to the King, Dean of Westminster 1605, Bishop of Rochester 1608, Lichfield and Coventry 1610, Lincoln 1614, Durham 1617, Winchester 1627, and Archbishop of York 1631. Died 1640.

[b] Sir Roger Owen, of Essex, knighted 1604. He was member for Shrewsbury, and took an active part in the violent proceedings of the House of Commons in the session of 1614. George Gerrard, writing to Carleton on 4th June, 1617, says he was seized with frenzy on hearing Lord Chief Justice Hobart argue the case of Commendams, and died in a week.—S.P.O. Dom. Corr. vol. xcii. 62.

[c] For the cause of the enmity which existed between the Kings of Sweden and Poland see note [b], page 84. The following circumstances will explain the ground of jealousy with Russia. Upon the deposition of the Emperor Basilius in 1610, in order to avoid the pretensions of the impostor Demetrius, the Russians conferred the crown upon Uladislaus, son of Sigismond III., King of Poland. This, however, was only to gain time. In 1613 the Russians revolted, drove out Uladislaus, and elected Michael Foederowitz Emperor. Two years afterwards Uladislaus made an attempt to recover the sovereignty, and a truce was entered into for 14 years, leaving the Duchies of Serevia, Czernicboro, and Novogrod, which the Poles had taken during the war, in their hands, and the permanent possession of these territories was confirmed by treaty in 1634.

The " Dragon " and the " Expedition " came safelye home out of the East Indies, but yett they are nott vnloaden.

Jvne.—The French Kinge declares himselfe overtlye to protect the Duke of Savoy agaynst the violence of Spayne, sayinge thatt yf he be vppressed he may nott suffer him to perishe, and an armye is levied readie vppon the frontier of Italie to marche in his ayde yf the Governour of Millan invade Piemont; but yf the Duke of Savoy will obstinattlye refuse to come to an indifferent and fayre agreement thatt he will then abandon him. June. Affairs of Italy.

This last monethe the Ladie Farmer,[a] daughter to Sir William Cornwallis, by mischance slew with a pistoll a gentleman called Onelye: she came to her triall to Newgatt, beinge indited of murther, but her answeres were nott vnlike to one distracted, wherevppon the judges respited judgment. Death of Mr. Onlay.

About 3 monethes past, the Erle of Abircorn's eldest sonne, whose surname is Hamilton, was created Baron of Strabane in Irland.[b]

Betwene the Turke and the Kinge of Pole there is no good intelligence; by the procurement of the great Signor 150,000 Tartares are in the fild to empeche the Poluckes desseygne in Moscovie, towards which territorie the Prince of Poland is marchinge with a competent armye. Affairs of Poland.

The Kinge of Sweden, havinge discovered thatt divers of his subiects had traffique withe the Kinge of Pole in the furtherance of his entended enterprise vppon Sweden, hathe cut of the bandes of some of the cheefest delinquents, and, to put the Polocke in despaire to be elected Kinge, hathe, accordinge to the forme of thatt countrie, caused himsellfe to be crowned*.

---

* He is nott yett crowned.

Cornelia, daughter and coheir of Sir William Cornwallis, by Lucy, third daughter and coheir of John Neville last Lord Latimer ; and wife of Sir Richard Fermor of Tusmore, co. Oxon: (Baker's Hist. of Northamptonsh. i. 599.) Chamberlain describes Mr. Onlay, " as a young dancing reveller of the Temple," who resorted much to Lady Formor.

b James, eldest son of James first Earl of Abercorn, who had large estates in Ireland; and this honour was conferred upon his son, being then only 13 years of age, to encourage his residence in that country. Upon the death of the Earl of Abercorn, in March 1618,

Itt is reported thatt the Frenche Kinge hathe caused an arrest to be made in Venice of 40,000 crownes which the Mareschall de Ancre had there in banke. There is allso in Amsterdam 17 great chestes of the Mareschall d'Ancre's arrested which were brought thether frome Reven, and were to have bene carried to Livorno: itt is thought thatt great store of money and iewells are in them.*

Fifteene hundred souldiours, levied in the Vnited Provinces for the Kinge of Sweden, are latelye embarqued, and are accompanied with 6 or 7 good shippes of warre.

The Count of Levenstein, a German, is presentlye to embarque att Amsterdam 3,000 foote, which he hathe levied in the ayde of the Venetians against the Archduke Ferdinand, commonlye called the Duke of Gratz: they are to pass the Strayts as the Count John of Nassav hathe done.

The Prince Mavrice his eldest base sonne, who was 16 yere olld, is latelye dead; his deathe is greatlye lamented, being a youthe of great expectation.

In revendge of the great spoyles which the Cossackes (who are protected by the Kinge of Pole) have done vppon the Turkes in the Black Sea, all by sea as vppon the maritime townes, the Grand Signor hathe sent an armye of 80 thousand horse and foote vppon the frontiers of Poland, whereby thatt kingdome suffers extreme calamities. To resist this great army the Kinge of Pole, with the ayde of some Christian princes his neyghbours, hathe levied great forces.

The Cantons of Bearne and Zuricke confederatt themselves with the Duke of Savoy agaynst the Spaniard, and they have sent to the Grisons to permitt passadge for 8,000 of there Swisses to pass vnto the Venetians ayde, whereunto they easilye assented, beinge more intimate vnto the State of Venice then vnto the Governour of Millan. Hetherto the Gazette from the Hage.

---

* This report of 17 chestes of the Mareschall d'Ancre's, is false.

Lord Strabane succeeded to the Earldom, and resigned the Barony to his brother Claude, but it subsequently merged again into the Earldom.—Nichols's Progresses of James I. vol. iii. pp. 382, 1102.

The Mareschall de Temines is latelye dead.

The Turkishe piratts dominier in the Mediterrane Sea, and our Turkish Pirates. marchants are daylye taken by them, in so muche as, yf the Christian princes do nott endevour there extirpation, the trade into the Levant willbe vtterlye destroyed.   In Spayne they spoyle the maritime villadges and take many prisoners, which is principallye affected by the banished Moores that once inhabited the easterne coast of Spayne. It is to feared that these piratts, which now are become good mariners, will visite ere itt be longe the christian coastes upon the ocean.

The Duke of Ossvna, Viceroy of Naples, is commanded (as itt is reported) to recall his shippes sent into the Gulphe of Venice, wherevppon the Venetians do recall there armada, which was att sea, to attend his attempts.

To the contrarye of this last above written intelligence, itt is affirmed, by lettres newlye arrived frome Venice, thatt the Duke of Ossvna's fleet, consisting of 12 gallions, 19 gallies, and 4 galliotts, of which sayed galliotts one Capten Eliott, our countryman, and an ancient sea capten, is commander, lye still in safe road ncere vnto Ragusa; that the Duke of Ossvna hathe sent a present of a shippes loadinge of Turkishe slaves to the Grand Signor ransome free; thatt he invites him to attempt the winninge of Candia, assuringe him thatt he will keep the Venetian sea forces from passinge out of the Gvllphe to him any impediment.

The 12. of this monethe Sir Walter Raleghe sett sayle att Pli- Raleghe's Expedition. mouthe.   God send him a prosperous retourne!   His fleet consists of 7 good shippes of warre and 3 pinnaces; he is excellentlye well manned, munitioned, and victualled, and will be able to land 6 or 700 men, his shippes beinge guarded.

Madame de Ancre hathe receved her triall, and is sentenced to be Trial of Madame d'Ancre. gvilltie of Sorcerie, Judaisme, and Peculate, which is stealinge or pourloyninge the Kinges money, and was adiudged to be hanged and burnt.

The 26. of this monethe I saw lettres which came from Venice, Affairs of Italy.

which report thatt the Venetian armada in the Gulphe or Adriatique
Sea have encountred with the Spanishe fleet, and of them they have
sunke 2 galleons, and taken 2 gallies of Naples,* but the reporte
speakethe of a greater victorie.   In these lettres itt is likewise
affirmed thatt nottwithstandinge the Duke of Ossvna's present of
slaves to the Grand Signor, and instead of attemptinge any thinge
vppon the Isle of Candia, he hathe comanded his Capten Bassa to
geve his attendance with 70 gallies and 10 shippes of warre to attend
the Venetian generall in the Gvllphe, and to be disposed by him
agaynst the Spaniard,† besides the sayed Bassa hathe commission to
draw into Albania 10,000 souldiers (as a further ayd) yf need required
itt.   A Holland shippe with 200 souldiars bound for Venice fell into
the Spanishe fleet, but suche was the Hollanders' resistance and dex-
teritie thatt the shippe recovered Ragusa, from whence they marched
to Cataro, and there is no dowbt of there safe comminge to the
Venetian army, which lies att the siedge of Gradisca.   The Spaniards
demanded these souldiars of the Ragusans, who, denienge there demand, in revendge they spoyled the countrie about the towne even
to the walls.   In the Haven they tooke the Holland shippe, hanged
the master, and made the mariners slaves.   The Venetian armye are
masters of the filld, and lye close to Gradisca, and have planted there
batterie, and in the hope to winne itt.   The Archduke's Generall
Tranmansdorffe is slayne.   Vercelly, a towne of the Duke of Savoyes,
is beseedged by the Spaniards, nevertheless the Duke hathe 3 tymes put
succours into itt.   The Marques of Caluzo, the governour of the towne,
in the sight of the beseedgers, vppon the wall of the towne hanged
the Podesta, the principall magistrate of Vercelli, because he vsed per-
swasions to the inhabitants to render themselves vnto the Spaniards.
The towne is well manned, and provided of all things, so as itt is
thought thatt the governour of Millan will fayle in the enterprise.

* For the sinkinge and takinge of these galleons and gallies, bonfires were made in
Venice, but there was no suche victorie, or any incountre by sea.
† This newes is vncertayne, but it is sure that the Turke is well inclined to assist the
Venetians.

The Archduke Ferdinand of Gratz, with all the nobillitie of Stiria, Affairs of Germany. Carinthia, and Croatia, and allso accompaned with the' Archduke Maximillian, is gone to Brage to beginne the Diet, wherein himsellfe expectethe to be elected Kinge of Bohemia.

Since which tyme we are credible advertised thatt he is elected Kinge of Bohemia, and by degrees there is little dowbt to be made of his beinge Emperour.

Sir John Digbye is gone frome London to embarque himsellfe in Sir John Digby sent Ambassador to Spain. the west countrie for Spayne; but the marriage so muche bruted betwene the hopefull Prince and the Infanta remaynes dowbtfull.

Julye.—The Marquise d'Ancre is executed; her head was cut of, July. Madame d'Anore exccuted. and her bodye burnt to ashes.

About the latter end of this last monethe Sir John Egerton, General news. Vicecount Brackeley, had his lettres pattents delivered vnto him for his Erldome of Bridgwater, so as now he is a confirmed Erle.

The Englishe councellers which attended the Kinge into Scotland are all of theme sworne councellers of thatt realme.

Sir John Herbert, the ancient Secretary of Estate,[a] is dead.

The Archduke Ferdinand of Gratz is crowned Kinge of Bohemia, Foreign news. and makes itt his steppe to the kingdom of the Romans, and so to the Empire. He is an obstinatt Papist Jesuited, and will nott permitt a Protestant into his house or court to serve him.

The Cossackes (who are an vnregular people dwellinge betwene Evrope and Asia and in the Ilands in the Black Sea, and vnder the protection of the Kinge of Poland,) have gevinge suche a great overthrow vnto the Turkes in the Blacke Sea as it dothe in a manner destroy the trade betwene the Tartares and the Turkes. The Grand Signor is muche troubled with itt, for itt diverts his sea forces frome doinge of any exploytes in the Mediterran Sea.

Gradisca is nott yett wonne by the Venetians, nor Vercelli by the Spaniards; they are, as of longe tyme they have bene, closelye besiedged, but nether of them as yett taken.

---

[a] He was second, or under, Secretary of State in 1603.

CAMD. SOC.   Q

The Turke hathe latelye sent an ambassador to the Emperour to require him to deliver vnto him sixty villages in Hungaria, wrongfullye (as he sayethe) detayned from him. Yf he refuse the request he threatens warre; and, like a prince that would be satisfied when his ambassador was dispatched, an army of 24,000 Turkes were sent into Hungary presently to destroy the Emperour's territories there. Whatt effects this ambassage will produce tyme will discover.

After a longe siedge, and muche bloode shed on ether side, Vercelli is rendered to the Spaniard by composition; the articles are honourable, as is reported. The losse of itt is a great blow to the Duke of Savoy.

Gradisco is relieved with men and victualls by the Archduke Ferdinand—I should have sayed the Kinge of Bohemia; and little hope remaynes thatt the Venetians' forces will carry itt. Neverthelesse the siedge continews.

ugust.

August.—The newes from Venice is thatt the Duke of Ossvna, Viceroy of Naples, hathe taken three gallies of the Venetians, bound for Spalato in Dalmatia. One of them was light; the other two loaden with goodes of Jewes, Turkes, Greekes, and Armeniens, to the valew of 1,000,000 of crownes. Further itt is sayed thatt the Venetian Armada lies in the porte of Lesina, nott daringe to looke outt, althoughe itt be composed of twelve shippes of warre, six gallyasses, and forty gallies. The Duke of Ossvna's fleet consists of eighteen gallions and thirty-three gallies. It is thought thatt the Venetians are in great danger of present rvyne, for yf the Duke of Savoy should accord to a peace with Spayne then thatt armye now employed vppon him would fall vppon the Venetian territories. The Kinge of Bohemia vexethe them with a warre in Istria, and the Duke of Ossvna lockes them vppe in the Gulphe, whereby there trade ceassethe, and succours helld from them. Neverthelesse the Count Leveinstein is now readie to embarque in the Low Countries 3,000 foote in fifteen good shippes in there ayde. God send him

good successe, for the attempt is brave and honourable! The dis-
coursers say thatt the Venetians must be enforced to call in the
Turke to there ayde, and to pay an yerelye tribute, as Ragusa dothe,
for his protection, *sed meliora spero.*

The Kinge of France (as it is sayed) hathe bestowed vppon
Mounsieur de Lvines the marquisatt of Ancre, and with itt of plate,
householldstuffe, money, and iewells of the dead marques, to the
valew of 800,000 crownes.

The Marquis Hamilton of Scottland is sworne a counceller of
England. He tooke his oathe at Glasco when the Kinge was there.

In Italye there is a generall feare of the Turkes invasion in thatt
territorie; tó resist the same all the shippes and gallies of Spayne,
Cicilie, and Malta, are assembled in the mouthe of the Gulphe of
Venice, and the fleet which the Duke of Ossvna hathe there to
annoy the Venetians are vnder the ensigne of the Kinge of Bohemia; for the Kinge of Spayne makes no overt warre agaynst them;
but his shippes, mariners, souldiars, and treasure are exposed in
thatt employment.

The Duke of Newbourge,[a] the pretender to Cleve and Juliers,
banishethe all Callvynists and Lutherans out of his territorye in the
Palatinatt, and admitts of none other then Romishe Papists. His
subiects which continew in there religion sell there patrimonies and
vndergoe exile.

The Venetians are in great feare of the Spanishe armada, which
daylie encreasethe; and they are so straightened as hardlye any
succours, ether by land or sea, cane come vnto them.

It is reported thatt the Emperor, the Kinge of Bohemia, the
Elector of Collogne, and the Duke of Saxe, have agreed vppon an

---

[a] Wolfgang William, Elector of Newburg, son of Philip Lewis, who claimed Juliers,
Berg, and Ravenstein, in right of his mother, one of the daughters and coheirs of
William Duke of Julich, Cleve, and Berg. The dukedom had passed by the marriage of
her elder sister and coheir to the Brandenburg family. Wolfgang William embraced
the Romish doctrine in 1614, and seems to have exhibited all the zeal of a convert. He
died 1653.

enterview att Moraco in Baviera, where a consultation will be helld for the electinge of a Kinge of the Romans, which in all likelyhood will fall vppon the Kinge of Bohemia.

Of late there hathe bene an embargue in Spayne of more then fifty Holland shipps, and vppon complaynt vnto the States Generall they sent an expresse messendger to the Archduke lettinge him to vnderstand thatt yf he did nott presentlye procure there discharge, and full satisfaction for all there damages, thatt they would right themselves vppon the Kinge of Spaynes subiects. Whatt this is like to produce you may easilye iudge.

The Ambassador of Savoy, who came· to negociatt a league betwene the Vnited Provinces and his master, is retourned to the Duke, and hathe obtaynced of the States assurance of ayde in money, but the alliance is protracted vntil they see whether the Duke (Vercelli beinge left) will persevere in the warre, for itt is sayed thatt now the Kinge of Spayne is inclined to a peace, and offers fayrer conditions than ever he did. The feare the Venetians have of a peace in Savoy troubles them infinitlye, for in all like-lyhood the armye now imployed in Piemont will be turned vppon them.

Frome Gvinea and Angola two Holland shipps are latelye arrived att Amsterdam exceedinge richlye loaden, especially with copper, which mettall, before this tyme, I never heard to be in those parts.

The faction about religion in the Vnited Provinces daylye en-creasethe; itt is feared thatt yll consequences will ensue.

Raleghe's expe-dition.
Sir Walter Raleghe was first by fowle wether enforced to put into Fallmouthe; after thatt, beinge 40 leagues cleare offe the coast of England in his course to the southward, was by force of wether driven into the haven of Corke, in Irland, and in the storme one of his pinnaces was oversett with a sayle and lost in his sight.

Foreign news.
Vppon the succouringe of Gradisca with men, munition, and victuall, the Venetians rose frome the siedge, which continewed longe, many men lost before itt, and the Venetians consumed an infinitt masse of treasure in the enterprise. Gradisca is seated vppon the

River of Lizonzo, in Frivli; the other side of the river is the vtter-most towne of the Kinge of Bohemia's territorie.*

Frome all parts of Evrope intelligences concurre thatt the Kinge of Spayne hathe promised the Infanta (which the world supposed thatt he had resolved to have sent into England to be our Prince's wife,) vnto the King of Bohemia's sonne, his cosen and brother-in-law, but vntill we heare frome our ambassador or agent in Spayne the truthe will nott appeare.

Mareschall de Digueres is gone into Piemont with 8,000 foote and 1,200 horse; the horse is comanded by the Count d'Avvergne, and the Duke of Rohan goes a volontier in the armye: there is allso gone into Piemont, in the ayde of the Duke of Savoy, 3,000 Swisse of the Canton of Bearne, but Vercelli was lost before there arrivall.

The Ladie Bowes, Sir William Wraye's [a] sister, is latelye maried English news. to the Lord Darcie of the Northe; her sister nott many monethes past was maried to the Lord Riche. .

The Lord Rosse, vppon the soddayne, no man beinge privie to his departure, attended but with one servant, is gone into France; somme say itt is to fight; a few days will discover the mistery.[b]

* I meane the Archduke Ferdinand.

[a] Isabel, eldest daughter of Sir Christopher Wray, Speaker of the House of Commons, married first Godfrey Foljambe, Esq , secondly Sir William Bowes, Knight ; and thirdly John Lord Darcy. Her sister Frances was twice married, first to Sir George St. Paul, of Snarford, and secondly to Robert Rich, Earl of Warwick. Chamberlain, writing on 11th October, 1617, says, "The Lord Rich is said to be in great perplexity, or rather crazed in brain, to see himself overreached by his wife, who hath so conveyed her estate that he is little or nothing the better for her, and, if she outlive him, likely to carry away a great part of his. Her sister, the Lady Bowes, hathe dealt clean contrary, being lately married to the Lord Darcy of the North, and being a great estate, whole and entire, and refusing any jointure or other advantage, saying it is sufficient for her to have the honour without any hindrance to the house."—Birch, ii. 37.

[b] The cause of his quitting the country so suddenly was the disgraceful conduct of his wife, and her mother Lady Lake, in respect to the charges brought against the Countess of Exeter. He proceeded to Rome, where in January 1618 he was living in great privacy,

The Hollanders have discovered to the southward of the Strayghts of Magellen an open sea and free passadge to the south sea.

The Ladye Roxboroghe is gone to live in Scottland, and retournes no more to serve her Majestie; in her place the Ladie Elizabeth Gray [a] succeeds.

Foreign news.
The Kinge of Poland's armye, which was commanded by the Prince his sonne, is overthrowene by the Turcs and Tartares: the Prince fled into Podolia to rayse new forces, which proved vayne; wherevppon the Kinge frome all parts levies men with an intention to go in person into the filde.

The Kinge of Sweden latelye with 6,000 men beseedged Riga, in Livonia: the inhabitants are resolved to defend itt vntil they be succoured by the Kinge of Pole; whatt will be the successe tyme will produce. It is allso sayed thatt the Kinge of Sweden will by force restore the Duke of Curland [b] to his countrye, who this last yere was banished by the Kinge of Pole and confiscated. This Duke of Curland is a neere kinsman to her Majestie, and was in England att the Kinge of Denmarke's first beinge here: his territorye is in Livonia.

September.—The warre in Piemont, betwene the Kinge of Spayne and the Duke of Savoy, is reported to be ended and a peace concluded. The like is expected betwene the Kinge of Bohemia and the Venetians.

The Duke of Nevers, the Duchesse his wife,[c] there eldest sonne (S.P.O. vol. xcv. 5,) having embraced the Roman Catholic doctrines. In the following March he was at Tivoli, and afterwards he proceeded to Naples, where he is said to have died on the 27th of June, 1618. We find, however, that there was a brief in a cause between the Attorney General and him relative to some lands at Walthamstow in November of that year (S.P.O. vol. ooij. 20), and there was a rumour that he was alive as late as March 1623 (S.P.O. vol. cxxxix. 64.)

   [a] Lady Elizabeth Grey de Ruthyn.

   [b] Frederick, second Duke of Courland, 1587-1641. His mother was Anne, daughter of Albert VI. Duke of Mecklenburg, whose other daughter, Sophia, was wife of Frederick II. King of Denmark, and mother of Queen Anne of England.

   [c] Catherine of Lorraine, daughter of Charles de Lorraine, Duke of Maine, married to

the Prince of Rhetelois, and the Duke of Mayne, were all of them bitten with a madde dogge; they are in great feare whatt may be the event; they are gone to St. Vallery, in Picardie, to trye whether the ayre of the sea and sea sicknes may geve theme remedie; the dogge thatt bitt them was a little one of the Duchesses of Nevers

In France, Sillerye and Villeroy governe the affayres of state; the great men of the sword are little employed, wherewith they are nott well plesed. The Prince of Conde is still in the Bastille, where he hathe gotten his wife with child, but of his deliverance in hast there is no apparance.

The Kinges Majestie retourned to Woodstocke frome his longe progresse out of Scotland the 6. September. The Queene and the Prince mett him there; and Sir George's feast (which by reason of his iourney into Scotland was prorogued vnto the 13. of this monethe) was helld at Windesor, att the which no knight was made by reason thatt there was no roame voyde. ^{The King's return from Scotland.}

In August last great difference hathe fallen out betwene Sir Edward Cooke and his wife the Ladye Elisabeth Hatton, about the marriage of Fraunces Cooke, there yongest daughter, vnto Sir John Villiers, the father consentinge vnto itt, and the mother opposite. The Lords of the Councell have bene often troubled with complaynts on ether side. The yonge gentlewoman was stolen away by her mother; Sir Edward Cooke recovered her agayne; vppon complaynte of the mother she was sequestered to one of the Clarkes of the Counsell's house, but by lettres frome his Majestie delivered to her father. The Ladye Hatton, as is sayed, endeavoured to have taken the mayde by force frome her father, for the which she was comitted prisoner to an alderman's house in London; but att Windesor the gentlewoman in the presence of the Kinge was formallye and legallye contracted vnto Sir John Villiers, the Ladye ^{Difference between Sir Edward and Lady Coke.}

Charles de Gouzague, Duke of Nevers, 1599. Their eldest son was François de Paule de Gonzague-Cleves, called Duke of Rethelois. He was Governor of Champagne and Brie, and died before his father in 1622. The Duchess died 8th March, 1618, aged 33.—Anselme.

Hatton beinge then and yett vnder restraynt. Sir Edward geves with his daughter 10,000^{li} in money, and for her present mayntenance 2,000 markes per annum, and after his deathe 1,000^{li} of yerelye inheritance. Within two or three dayes followinge Sir Edward Cooke was restored agayne to his place in Counsell.

Renewed
hostilities
in Savoy. After longe debatinges about a peace betwene Spayne and Savoy, and when the intelligence in all parts was divulged thatt the peace was concluded, itt soddaynlye brake off. The Duke of Savoy presentlye marched into Montferratt, where he bathe taken one of the best townes in itt, and in the Duchye of Myllan he hathe taken two small townes; himsellfe commands one armye, and the prince his sonne another, with whom the Mareshall Digueres with his Frenche is ioyned. The fame goes thatt they have an intention to beseege Novara and Alexandria, two great citties garrizoned by the Spaniards.

Raleghe's expe-
dition. The 23. of this last monethe I heard frome Sir Walter Raleghe, in the heyght of the Northe Cape of Spayne; his fleet was thirteen sayle of all sorts, and 1,000 good men in them. He sett sayle out of Irland the 19. of August, where he repayred himsellfe with victualls and other necessaries whereof he stood in want. When he wrote he had a franke gale of wynd, and stood to the southward.

French news. Since the deathe of the Mareshall d'Ancre in France, Monsieur de Lvynes growes towards greatnes with no lesse speed then he did; and by the favour he hathe the Princes are no lesse kept vnder then in former tymes, so as vnto them itt appeares thatt the person of the man is onlye changed and nothinge ells. This new favourite strengthens himsellfe, and is latelye married to the Duke of Mombazon's daughter, with whom he had a great portion; and itt is thought that he shall be shortlye honnoured with the tittle of Duke and Peere of France. The Queene Mother lives a retired lyfe in Blois; her household is nott great, and but small resort vnto her.

The Prince of Conde is so farre frome beinge enlarged as thatt he is removed frome the Bastill to Bois de Vincennes, and good gvardes to assure him.

The princes of France are generally discontented; and the opinion rvnnes thatt ere itt be longe thatt realme will be in a tumult.

Our Turkie marchants resiant in Constantinople are yll entreated; many wronges are done them. They complayne and can fynde no justice, wherewith they are so muche discouraged as they are dowbtfull whether they shall continew thatt trade or relinquishe itt.

The Turkes and Tartares harrasse and spoyle the frontiers of Polonia. To confront them the Prince of Poland hathe an armye of 20,000, Solkoskye another of 18,000. The princes and noblesse of Podolia have a third armye of 15,000; these lye vppon the borders of Walachia and Podolia. The Cossackes with 40,000 lye vppon the confines (of) Tartarye, which armies are imployed to no other end then to restrayne the manifold incursions of the Turkes and Tartares. <abbr>Affairs of Poland.</abbr>

The Moscovitts of Smolenskie, wearye of the subiection they are in, are desirous to have the Prince of Poland for there lord.

The Emperour, the Kinge of Bohemia, the Archduke Maximillian, and others, have bene of late att Dresden with the Elector of Saxe, prayinge his furtherance for the election of the Kinge of Bohemia to be Kinge of the Romans. <abbr>Affairs of Germany.</abbr>

The siedge of the towne of Riga in Liffland is continued by the Kinge of Sweeden, and he hathe sent a commander with forces into the Duchye of Curland to mayntayne the possession of itt for him, for the which the Duke of Curland is to have lands in Sweden.

Otto [a] the sonne and heyre to the Lantzgrave of Hessen, shootinge a deare, and his peece faylinge to fire, to mend the defect, in turninge the mouthe of itt towards him, itt fired and shott him throughe the head, whereof he instantlye died.

The plague beginns to grow warme in the Low Countries; there hathe died in Amsterdam above 500 a weeke.

Seven Spanyshe shippes freyghted with souldiars for Italye were

---

[a] Otto, son of Maurice Landgrave of Hesse Cassel, born 1594. Died 7 August, 1617. He was twice married, but left no issue.

fought withall by the Turkyshe piratts; one was sunke, another taken, and 5 escaped by goodnes of sayle.

The Lord (Cobham?) for the betteringe of his healthe had his majesties leave to go to the Bathe attended by his keeper. In his retourne, beinge as he conceved throughlye cured of his maladie, was, at Hungerford, surprized with a dead palsey, frome thence with difficultie he was carried alyve vnto Odiam, Sir Edward Moore's house; he is yett livinge, but nott like to continew many dayes.

The Earl of Tirone,[a] thatt infamous traytor, had latelye in the Low Countries two sonnes; Shane the eldest is collonel of the Irishe regiment with the Archduke his yonger brother, Brian, was at Bruxells found hanged in his chamber with his hands bound behind him, but by whome this villaneous act was committed itt is nott knowne.

Death of Brian O'Neal.

Death of Sir Daniel Dunn.

Sir Daniell Dvn, who was Master of the Requests, Deane of the Arches, and Judge of the Admiraltie, is dead[b]; and so is Sir Bernard Dewhurst, a gentleman of your acquayntance.

When I was thus farre proceeded with this ydle gazette, which although itt be seriated by monethes yett you must nott geve creditt thatt all the thinges vnder the title of the monethe passed in the sayed monethe, for I sett theme downe as they came to my knowledge, whereof I thought itt good to ·geve you cavtion. But att this tyme, which was the 28. of September, I receved your lettre and relation or iournall, for the which I geve you infinitt thankes, beinge an assured testimonye of your love which shall nott be lefte vnmerited on my part in any thinge wherein I shall have the happynesse to manifest the love and affection I beare you.

Your lettre hathe filled me with many sad thoughts thatt I should be suche an unfortunatt frend as to preferre vnto your service suche a monstrous wretche as Jones hathe proved; the memorie of him is so hatefull vnto me, as I professe vnto you, these eyes of myne (yf they may avoyde itt) shall never see him, and yf I found him

---

[a] See note [c], p. 40.

[b] Chamberlain says that, " he died no rich man for all that he had three good offices."
—Birch, ii. 35.

starvinge in the streets I would nott afford him. Christian charitie to
save his lyfe. God, I hope, will never permitt him to retourne, for I
conceve him to be a limme of the divell and fitter to end his cursed
lyfe amonge Infidells then Christians. Forgeve my misfortune, for
itt afflicts me more than you can imagine, and I thanke you for re-
latinge his villanies vuto me in a privatt lettre, for I am ashamed to
have itt knowne thatt I did preferre him vuto you. As for his vnkle
I do assure you (vppon my faythe) thatt he holds him in no lesse
detestation then I do, and I am sorrye with all my harte thatt he was
nott hanged by the Kinge or you when his fillthenesse and treasons
towards you were manifested.

Lett me entreat you to be carefull to make the mappe of the
Mogolls territorie as you have intended; itt will be a worke worthye
of your sellfe, and adorne your travell and iudgement, and leave to
the world a lastinge memorie when you are dust. And allso to gett
the storye of thatt countrye to be translated, which in your relation
you say was offred to you by an old gentleman, the new Governour
of Syndv; the man I meane is he thatt feasted you in one of the
Kinges houses. I conceve thatt some Dutch, Portugaye, or Italian
inhabitant may be found to do itt, or, yf you fayle of suche, yf you
may gett some Persian to translate itt into his language, English
marchants will be found to putt itt into Englishe.

I do nott a little admyre of the greatnes of thatt monarque; the
description you make of the riches which you saw when he left
Adsmere exceedes all the reports thatt ever I read of, and yet I observe (in your discourse) more basenes in thatt prince and people
then canne be imagined where suche abvndance of earthlye treasures
are found.

The lettre you mention sent vnto me in your pacquett overland
miscaried. I never receved any suche, and yett I was very diligent
to seeke after itt, concevinge thatt you had remembred me as well
as you did other of your friends. Thatt pacquett was sent from
Aleppo to Constantinople, there opened by the ambassador, and all
the lettres were delivered to Mr. Porye, who brought them into

England: he assures me there was nott any directed vnto me, and
Sir Thomas Smythe (in like manner) protested the same after the
pacquet came into his hands, so as I know nott where to lay the
fault, and yet I amme sure there hathe beene some tromperye vsed.

Vnto me of your retourne you write nothinge, neverthelesse I
thinke as soone as this shippinge shall come vnto you you willbe the
messendger of your owne healthe, whiche I wishe with my hart;
for your tyme spent amonge infidells hathe bene sufficient, yf not
too muche.

In my last[a] vnto you I touched of a relation made by a frier of his
iourney frome Lahor by caravan vuto Pacquin or Cambalu in China,
and allso I discoursed somewhatt of the rivers of Indus and Ob, of
which rivers I do thinke you shall do well to informe your sellfe,
for the distance betwene them is nott muche, and they are bothe
of them great and navigable.

Vppon Christmas day the mariage betwene Mrs. Francis Cooke
and Sir John Villiers was solempnised att Hampton Court: the
bride was led to the chapple by the Prince and the Erle of Buckingham, and his Majestie did geve her. But the Ladye Hatton was
nott released frome the Alderman's guard, and therefore absent, and
so was the Erle of Exeter and all his familie.

The Lord Willoughbye of Parhame is dead.[b]

October. *October.*—The faction in the Vnited Provinces about ecclesias-
tique conformitie workes a great distraction in those parts, some of
the townes professinge themselves Arminians, wherein they are so
violent as itt is like to produce fearefull events. Barnevault is an
obstinatt Arminian, and, havinge bene latelye sent for by the Estats
Generall to come to the Haghe, he hathe refused to obey the summons, wherevppon he is helld in great suspition; and, whereas one
of his sonnes was Governour of Bergen ap Zome, the States in their
providence have ioyned a joint commander in thatt government with

_____

[a] See pp. 52, 63.   [b] William Willoughby third Lord.

him. Many of the townes in Holland and ellswhere, for their bettre securitie in this increasinge distraction, att the proper towne chardges, have erected companies for their saftie. The townes of Rotterdam, Leyven, Harlem, Tergaw, and sundrye others, as Vtrecht, &c., do apparantlye professe themsellves to be Arminians. To vphold the reformed Church, prince Mavrice resorts to sermons more then accustomed, and to suppresse the fire kindled he iourneys to all the places most suspected, to put good gvards vppon them. These devisions, vnlesse God in his mercye prevent itt, will shortlye breake out into open combustions, and open a fayrre way for the Pope and Spayne.

The Turkishe piratts have this sommer beene vppon the coastes of England and Irland; but they have done no hurte, allthoughe itt was in there power, for betwene Vshant and Syllye they mett with fishermen and barques loaden with fishe, of whom they bought commodities, payinge for them more then the wares was worthe, whiche makes me to conceve thatt this yere they came but to discover and view the coaste; but hereafter this, I amme afrayd, we shall have to much of there custome and lesse civillitie. Latelye these circumcised piratts, nott farre frome the Northe Cape of Spayne, tooke three Spanishe shippes bound for France. Itt is sayed thatt in them of readie money there was above the some of 60,000^{li} sterlinge. Turkish pirates.

Mrs. Elizabeth Bridges, or Ladye Kenedie,[a] my Lord Chandos cosen german, was latelye svrprised with a dead pallsie, whereof in a few dayes, the 7 of this monethe, she died.

Doctor Mountayne,[b] the Deane of Westminster, is to be bishoppe of Lincoln.

[a] Elizabeth, the youngest of the two daughters and heirs of Giles Brydges, third Lord Chandos, and widow of Sir John Kennedy. She was born 1577. She is supposed to be " fair Mrs. Bridges " with whom the unfortunate Earl of Essex fell in love, (Sidney Papers, vol. ii. 90,) which probably caused Queen Elizabeth " to use her with words and blows of anger," and to banish her the court for three days. Chamberlain says " she died very poor, her maintenance being little or nothing but as it were the judicious alms of her friends."—Birch, ii. 41.

[b] Dr. George Mountaigne, one of the King's Chaplains, Dean of Westminster, 1610-17. Bishop of Lincoln 1617-21, London 1621-28, Durham 1628, Archbishop of York 1628. Died soon afterwards.

The Lord Gerrard,[a] Lord President of Wales, is dead; his successor is yett vnknowne.[b]

Affairs of Poland and Russia. The Kinge of Poland workes all the meanes he may to grow to a pacification with the Turke to geve his sonne the prince a fayre way to accommodate the affayres of Moscovie, betwene whome and the now Emperor of Russia there is a treatie for surrenderinge his estate to the prince. The Emperor, as itt seemes, is wearye of thatt government, and is contented to resigne the same, so as he may have other possessions transferred vppon him, whereby he may live in the qualitie of a prince. He likewise desires thatt his father, who is a prisoner in Polonia, may be enlarged and sent home. To prosecute this busines the prince is nott slow, havinge allreadie raysed 60,000 souldiars to passe into Moscovia.

Affairs of Germany. It is reported that shortlye a diet will be held att Ratisbone for the election of a Kinge of Romans.

The Kinge of Sweeden, with 22,000 in his armye, lies still before Riga, and the towne is reduced to suche extremities as itt cannott longe holld out: the Kinge of Poland hathe attempted to relieve itt bothe by land and sea, but he fayled in ether, his land companies beinge defeated, and 5 of his shippes, loaden with munitions and other provisions, taken.

The Kinge attempted to take the towne of Pernav in Liffland, but fayled in the enterprise.

The plague att Collen, Munster, Amsterdam, and especiallie in the townes of Hennallt and Arthois, daylye encreasethe and spred ittsellfe allmost all over the Lower Germanie.

Great levies of men are made in Germanye, as well by the Emperor and the Kinge of Bohemia as by the Electours spirituall and temporall, and by all the rest of the princes of either religion. Whatt will be the event of these preparations, or to whatt end they are made, is yett vnknowne, every man havinge his particular censure. The Arch-

---

[a] Thomas first Lord Gerard. See n. ᵉ, p. 91. Chamberlain says that he enjoyed that place but a little, nor his fair young lady.—Birch, vol. ii. p. 35.

[b] It was given to Lord Compton.

duke in his territories dothe the like, and the Vnited Provinces
strengthen there frontiers, havinge allso geven forthe there com-
mandments thatt all suche as are intertayned by them shall be in a
readiness to draw into the fylde as occasion shall require.

The territories of Collen, Treves, and Ivilliers are extremelye Plague of rats.
afflicted with innumerable troopes of ratts, which devoure all the
frutes, as well housed as growinge in the gardens and fillds, and
especially the vines are destroyed by them, so thatt great dearthe is
feared to ensue in those parts, and besides itt is holld for an yll
pressage of future calamitie.

The treatie of peace betwene Spayne and Savoy is renewed The war in
agayne, and the Kinge of Spayne, now att the last, is contented to Italy.
confirm the conditions agreed vppon att Asti, which, as I remember,
was published before your departure out of England; but betwene
the last treatie, which soddenlye brake of, and this which I now
speake of, the Duke of Savoy bathe bene victorious, havinge in
this interim taken fyve stronge places frome the Spaniard, 14 ensignes, and slayne and taken of his enemies above 4500.

Of the Prince of Condies enlargement there is lesse hope then
ever; he is still prisoner in Bois de Vincennes, gvarded by 600
souldiars of the continued regiments, who are comanded by Monsieur Cadenet, a brother to the favorite de Lvynes.

There is great workinge in France for the recallinge of the French news.
Queene Mother to the court, but the Kinge geves a deaf care vnto itt.

Of late a gentleman, an ordinarie attendant vppon the Frenche
Kinge, as the Kinge was goinge to the duke of Vendosmes house to
christen his chilld, advised his Majestie to take good care of himsellfe,
for thatt the duke had a purpose to poyson hym, wherevppon the Kinge
retourned, to the great amazement of the duke and all others: thatt
done, he went to the Duke and told him thatt the Kinge was advertised thatt he should have bene poysoned by him, and therefore he
wished him to preserve his life by present flight, for the Kinge
had a purpose to seeze vppon his person: the Duke's innocencye
bred confidence in him, and would nott bouge. The Kinge and his
counsayle were different in opinion whether vppon the information

the Duke should be arrested, but in the end, because in him there appeared no apparence of feare, his arrest was differred.   The gentleman, seeinge thatt his practize did not succeed as he had imagined, bent his mallice agaynst Vendosme, and to make good his information to the Kinge, he practised with three or four others of the souldiars of the gvardes, who confirmed his accusation, but one of these conspirators revealed the plott to the Duke, who presentlye went to the Kinge, and, the matter beinge called into examination, the practize agaynst Vendosme evidentlye appeared, wherevppon the gentleman thatt had framed this impious fallshood was publiquelye executed.

In Paris a groome of the Marques de Rosny his chamber, beinge broken vppon the wheele for a rape, voluntarylye confessed, but how trulye I know nott, thatt his master the Marques had practised with him for the poysoninge of his wife, who is Monsieur de Crecqui his daughter, and thatt a burgesses wife in Paris, whome the Marques loved, should do as moche for her husband, and then, beinge on ether part free, a marriage betwene them was agreed vppon.   Whether this report be trew or fallse, itt is a misfortune for the Marques to have suche a scandell cast vppon him, and itt will be the more easilie beleeved, because betweene him and his wife there is no very good agreement.   The Duke of Svlly, his father, is muche afflicted with itt.

The Count John Ernest of Nassav, who the last (year) carried a Netherland regiment in the ayde of the Venetians, is latelye dead att Venice.

Home news.   In the roome of the Lord Gerrard, latelye deceased, Lord Compton[a] is constituted Lord President of Walles.

Sir Thomas Mowtas, who, as you know, was a gentleman of an able and stronge constitution, nott beinge formerlye sicke, died soddaynlye,* and so did your olld acquayntance Silvanus Skorye,[b] Sir

* This is false, but Skorie is dead.

---

[a] William second Lord, created Earl of Northampton 1618.

[b] Sylvanus Soory in 1615 proposed a scheme for enlarging the privileges of Baronets, suggesting that they should be relieved from wardship, be justices of the peace at 21 years of age, deputy-lieutenants, their bodies to be free from arrest, with several other immunities—to be granted upon a payment of 3,000l.

John Parker,[a] the gentleman Pentioner and Capten of the forte att
Fallmouthe is dead, and Sir Robert Killygrew is his successor at
Fallmouthe.

The 8. of September last Sir Wallter Raleghe came to an anchor Raleghe's expe-
att the Ilaud of Lanzarota, as you know, one of the Isles of the dition.
Canaries, frome whence one Capten Baylye, who commanded in a
shippe of 100 tonnes, stole frome him and is retourned: the cause of
his abandoninge the flecte he alleadgethe to be the feare he had
thatt Sir Walter would turne piratt, but he dothe nott charge him
with any fact comitted. I do thinke in the end he will be sorry and
ashamed bothe of his retourne and for the skandell which his report
hathe cast vppon his generall; in the meane tyme there is a dowbtfull
opinion helld of Sir Wallter, and those thatt mallice him boldlye
affirme him to be a piratt, which, for my part, I will never beleeve.

The newes from the Haghe is thatt the Prince of Poland, invited News from the
by sundrye of the grandes of Moscovie, is gone thether to be enstalled Hague.
in thatt empire, but gvarded with a convenient army.

We heare frome Spayne thatt Sir John Digbye, his Majesties Am-
bassadour, hathe bene royallye receved by the Kinge and his grandes;
but yett nothinge is negotiated about the employment for the which
he was sent.

Sir Robert Sherlye is arrived att Lisbone, but he is nott admitted
to come to the Court, and is appoynted to treat with the viceroy of
Portugall about his negotiation; his brother Sir Anthonye[b] is att

---

[a] Sir John Parker was granted the office of Keeper of Falmouth (Pendennis) Castle for
life, March, 1607. (S. P. O. Index Warrant Book, p. 56.)

[b] Sir Anthony and Sir Robert Sherley were sons of Sir Thomas Sherley of Wiston, co.
Sussex. For an account of their adventurous lives see Nichols's Leicestershire, vol. iii.
pp. 722-727, and The Sherley brothers, an Historical Memoir of the Lives of Sir Thomas,
Sir Anthony, and Sir Robert Sherley, edited (chiefly from documents in the State-Paper
Office) by Evelyn Philip Shirley, esq., and presented by him in 1848 to the Roxburghe
Club. Sir Robert was long resident in Persia, where he married Teresia, daughter of
Ismael Khan, a Circassian Christian of noble birth. His wife accompanied him to
England, where she gave birth to a son in 1611, at whose baptism Prince Henry and
the Queen were sponsors. On Sir Robert's return to Persia in 1613 he bequeathed the
child to the favour and care of her Majesty.

Madrid, exceedinge poore, yett he hathe 3000 ducatts pention by the yere, but 2000 of them is by the justice imbargued towards the payment of his debtes.

Death of Sir Ralph Win-wood.

This 28. day of October Sir Rallphe Winwood, his Majesties Secretarie, died of a burninge fever, whereof he laye nott sicke above 6 dayes; he died at his house in the great St. Bartholomews, in London.

Moorish pirates.

The Moores of Spayne, banyshed as you know some few yeres past into Barbarye, havinge latelye encreased in shippinge, infest the coast of Spayne, spoylinge weake maritime townes; they have allso bene att the Canaries and Madera, where they have made havoke, and taken above 2000 prisoners; there strength att sea is more then 60 shippes. This was advertised from the Haghe the 25. of this monethe.

Affairs of Ger-many.

Nottwithstandinge the peace concluded, as is sayed, betwene the Kinges of Spayne, Bohemia, and the Venetians, the Count of Leven-stein, before mentioned, is gone from Holland with his regiment of auxilliaries in the ayde of the Venetians: he embarqued his men att Dellfziel.

The Emperor's Ambassador, in retourninge frome Constantinople, was (with all his retinew) taken prisoner by the Turkes, first carried to Buda, and from thence to Bellgrado, kept with a sure gvard. Vppon report of this affront the Emperour hathe imprisoned the Turks Ambassador and his retinew in Vienna.

Hungarie is all in disorder, nothinge but warre is expected, and itt is sayed thatt the Emperor will in person presentlye go into Hungarie to sett some order in thatt kingdome.

November. Home News.

November.—The first of this monethe the Lady Hatton, havinge formerlye made her submission to his Majestie, wherein he was well pleased, was enlardged of her restraynt, and brought to her father's house, beinge honorablye attended by sundry noble and great per-sonadges, and nott onelye she applauded the marriage of her daughter vnto Sir John Villiers, but itt is thought she will geve all her purchased lands, which is bettre then 2000 li. by the year (after her lyfe) vnto her daughter and her heyres.

Sir Henry Riche,[a] vppon the resignation of the vicecount Fenton, is now Capten of the Gvard.

The Lord Hay is maried vnto the Ladye Lucye Percy, the Erle of Northumberland's daughter.

The Bishoppe of Hereford, Doctor Bennett, is dead; Godwine,[b] Bishoppe of Landaffe, is his successor, and Doctor Charleton,[c] the prince's chaplain, succeeds him.

There is a report from Venice (which I feare is to trew) thatt a yonge kinsman of myne, called Francis Carew,[d] the eldest sonne to Sir George Carew the late Master of the Wardes, is taken by the Turkishe piratts in passinge betwene Ligorno and Spayne: you know the boy, for he went with the Electresse into Germanye.*

Thoughe the peace was sayed to be concluded betwene the Venetians and the Kinges of Spayne and Bohemia, yett as soone as the Duke of Savoy had disarmed, the Spanishe troopes marched into the Venetians territories, and burnt and harassed some villadges. Whatt new flame this may kindle after times will discover. *Renewed hostilities in Italy.*

The Hollanders this sommer have attempted once more the discoverye of the northwest passage by Fretum Davis, and itt is reported thatt all the difficulties are past. In this discoverye they found a nation of pigmeis; two of them they tooke in a small canoe. When they had brought them abord there shippe, the cooke was *North-west passage.*

* I thanke God this report is proved fallse, for he is safelye arryved in Spayne.

----

[a] See note [a], p. 38.

[b] Dr. Francis Godwin, son of Thomas Godwin, Bishop of Bath and Wells from 1561. He was author of De Præsulibus Angliæ Commentarius, &c. and other works. Bishop of Llandaff 1601, Hereford 1617, died 1633.

[c] Dr. George Carleton, Bishop of Llandaff 1617, Chichester 1619, died 1628, aged 69.

[d] He was created K.B. at the coronation of Charles I. In the same year we find that he was a prothonotary in Chancery, payment having been made to his deputy Humphrey Roberts for engrossing and ornamenting various public instruments of great importance, amongst them the King's marriage articles (S. P. O. Dom. Corr. Chas. I. vol. xiii. 78.) In 1628 he was connected with a proposition for the defence of the Isles of Scilly (Ibid. vol. xci. 105) in which year he died.

dressinge a piece of porke, which they percevinge, concevinge itt to be man's fleshe, and fearinge (as is conceved) to be devowred, bothe of them lept into the sea, and so drowned. How farre the Hollanders entred into Fretum Davis, or what course they helld, I do nott know, and this storie of the pigmeis I have but by relation, but I do thinke itt to be trew.

Home news. The 30. day of this monethe, the Ladye Markham, wyfe to Sir Griffithe Markham (who yett lives), for maryenge one of her servants together with her late husband, did pennance in white sheets at Pawles Crosse; the like they must do at Yorke and ellswhere, and are fyned in 1000 li. How they escaped deathe (as the statute lately made [a] for thatt offence providethe) I cannott well deliver, and yett they were arraygned for itt vppon thatt statute.

Monsieur de Lvynes, the French Kinges especial privado, is now confirmed governour of Normandie.

The Electresse Palatine, our soverayne's onely daughter, is great with child. God send her a happie deliverance of another sonne! [b]

The last of this monethe the Archbishop of Spalato preached att the Mercers' chapple in London, in the Italian tonge, with infinite applause of his avditors.

In this monethe there came a Moscovie ambassador to the Kinge, the best attended and with the richest presents of furres thatt ever I saw come frome thence.

December. *December.* —The first of this monethe Arthur Wingfilld,[c] the Countesse of Bedford's cosen germayne, and my kinsman (who was once her page, and after thatt (yf I be nott mistaken) a servant to the Ladye Electresse her grace, and lastlye a gentleman attendant vpon Prince Mavrice,) was slayne in privatt dvel by a yonge gentleman called Ayllyff, a Wiltshire man: Wingfilld was left dead in the place, and the other is now a prisoner. Wingfilld's second is fled,

[a] 1 Jac. I. cap. 11.   [b] See note, [a] p. 136.
[c] See note [a], p. 65.

and Ayllyffe will hardlye escape the rigor of the law, the Kinge
beinge a professed enemie to duells, and therefore little hope of
favour is lefft for dvellistes.

Sir Edward Villiers (a brother to the Erle of Buckingham, by his
father) hathe the place in the mynt which Sir Richard Martin [a] had:
itt is thought to be worthe 1,500 or 2,000 li. by the yere; some
thinke itt to be of bettre valew, but the quallitie of thatt office is
bettre or worse accordinge to the masses of money which is coyned.

Capten Harvey, who was three yeres with Harecourt in Gviana, Expedition to
is gone agayne to trye a fortune there; the river of Weyapoco,[b] nott Guiana.
(as you know) above two degrees from the Lyne, is the first harbo-
roughe thatt he meanes to fall withall; he is victualled for eleven
monethes, shipt in a bottome of 200 tonnes and 70 men; his shippe
he meanes to retourne as speedilie as he may, and with the rest of his
men to stay there.

Monsieur de Villeroy, the ancient and famous Secretary of France, Death of Ville-
is dead.　　　　　　　　　　　　　　　　　　　　　　　　　　roy.

The warres betwene the Kinge of Spayne and the Duke of Savoy, Affairs of Italy.
which by the late treatye was thought to be finallye ended and com- .
posed, is like to breake forthe into new hostillitie, for the Kinge of
Spayne (as the Duke sayethe) dothe not perfourme his part of the
conditions, refusinge to render the towne of Vercelli vntill all the
townes in Monferratt (now possessed by the Duke) be delivered into
his hands, which, by the treatie, ought to be delivered vuto the
Duke of Mantua.

Formerlye I recounted vnto you, thatt one Capten Baylie (a Raleghe's Ex-
capten in Sir Walter Raleghes fleet) was retourned into England, pedition.
and gave out reports thatt Sir Wallter was, or would, turne piratt.
Since which tyme one Reekes, a master dwellinge in Ratcliffe, who
was at Lanzarote all the tyme thatt Sir Wallter was there, beinge
examined, reportethe thatt Sir Wallter, after he had landed 400

---

[a] Sir Richard Martin was goldsmith to Queen Elizabeth and Warden of the Mint in
her reign.　In 1604 he was Master of the Mint, and so continued until his death.

[b] River Oyapok.

men, sent to the governour to pray him free libertie to water, and
to furnisshe himsellfe of suche necessaries as he wanted for his
money.   The gouvernour and he mett, many complements passed
betwene them, and promised thatt he should want nothinge which
the iland did afford.   The next day Sir Wallter sent vnto him agayne,
and so the third day; in the end when all the goodes in the towne of
Lanzarota was sent to the mountaynes, and the weemen and chill-
dren in saftie, he sent him word thatt he was a piratt, and thatt he
should have no more there then whatt he could wynne by his
sword.   In this mean tyme, some of Sir Wallter's men, contrary to
his directions, stragglinge into the countrye, were slayne; two dead
in the place, and the third escaped with 16 woundes.   Notwith-
standinge this afront and yll dealinge, Sir Wallter, beinge carefull
nott to transgresse his commission (contrarye to the desire of all his
captens) repayred to his shippes without revendge.   From thence
he went to water att the grand Canárie, and, as his men were busie
in there labour in fillinge of caske, the gouvernour assayled them,
drove them to there boates, with the losse of one of the saylers: in
reskew of them Sir Wallter Ralegh made a shot out of his shippe
in a great peece, and slew one of the Spaniards, which done he
hoysed sayle and went to the island of Gomera, where he was well
intreated and furnisshed himsellfe of water and other comodities
which he wanted, and from thence about the 20. of September he
sett sayle for the Indies, since which tyme we have not heard of him.

Home news.   Doctor Felton [a] and Doctor Mountayne [b] were att Lambethe consecrated Bishoppes, the one of Bristow and the other of Lincolne.

Judge Snygge,[c] one of the Barons of the Exchequer, is dead.

---

[a] Dr. Nicholas Felton, President of Pembroke Hall, Cambridge. He was translated to
Ely 1619.   Died 1626, aged 63, and was buried in the church of St. Antholin, London,
of which he had been formerly Rector.

[b] See note [b], p. 15.

[c] George Snigge, Serjeant at Law 1603, Baron of the Exchequer 1604. He was
granted the office of Judge of the Circuit for the counties of Glamorgan, Brecon, and
Radnor, May 13, 1608, being then a knight.—S. P. O. Docquet.

The newes in Germanye is, that themperour beinge contynualye News from Germany. sicklye and not like to lyve, is desirous in his lyfe tyme to invest his cosen the Kinge of Bohemia into the Kingdóme of Hungarie, to make him a farther steppe to the title of Kinge of the Romans, and to thatt end allso he hathe sent to the secular Electors to repayre vnto him to conferre vppon thatt busines, but itt is sayed thatt the Electors of Rhyne [a] and Brandenburge [b] have made civill excuses.

The siedge of Riga is still continued by the Kinge of Sweden, and driven to great extremities.

The Prince of Poland, in hope to be receved as Great Duke, entred into Russia, but his frends fayled him, and there he hathe received a defeate.

The marriage betwene the Lantzgrave of Hesses daughter with Count Henry of Nassav is still helld in treatye, but nott yett thoroughlye concluded.

In the Vnited Provinces there is a nationall synode appoynted to be helld at Dort in May next, for the appeasinge and settlinge of the differences in religion.

The Kinge of France is latelye come to Paris frome Roane, where French news. there hatho a great assemblye (but not the full bodye of the three estates, yett certayne persons delegated) for every province and cittie in France, wherein many reformations hathe bene made, and amonge the rest, to forbidde a custome overmuche frequented, itt was ordayned thatt from thenceforthe none of the Kinges subiects should comunicatt or receve lettres from ministers of forrayne states as agents or ambassadors. The Cardinall of Peronne [c] pressed hard thatt the Popes Nvnce might be excepted, but itt was reiected, whereatt the Nvnce was in an extreme rage and greevous complaint, but without redress.

---

[a] Frederick V. Elector Palatine.

[b] John Sigismund, born 1572, Elector 1608. He made a public profession of the Reformed religion 1614. Died 1619.

[c] Jacques Davi du Perron, Bishop of Evreux and Archbishop of Sens, Grand Almoner of France, made Cardinal 1604. Died 1618.

The Princesse of Conde, who remaynes with her husbande in prison, is lately delivered of an abortive sonne, which hathe renewed the publique complaynts against the hard proceedinge towards him.

The French, in generall, speake brodlye of the Spaniards cavtelous delayes in nott renderinge of Vercelli to the Duke of Savoy, and the Kinge professethe thatt yf the Spaniards do nott perfourme the treatie exactlie, thatt he will shew himsellfe in the busines in the Dukes part.

News from Constantinople.

The newes from Constantinople is, thatt the vizier Bassa is overthrown by the Persian, in which defeate of 150,000 Turkes 20,000 escaped. Allthoughe the truthe of this is bettre known vuto (you) then vs, yett I thought itt nott vnmeet to lett you know whatt ronnes currant here.

It is allso reported frome thence thatt the Cossakes have defeated 12,000 Turkes, and there chief commander taken prisoner, whome they sent as a present vuto the Kinge of Polonia, and nott ceassinge they made by sea an incursion into the empire of Trebisond, burninge and spoylinge a great number of townes and villadges, which hathe moved suche a passion in the Grand Signor as he purposes to employ all his indevour for there extirpation.

Home news.

The 29. of this monethe the Kinge had intelligence thatt the Princesse Electresse his daughter was delivered of another sonne [a] (whom God blesse).

The 30. the Lord Clifton,[b] for castinge forthe some speeches thatt he had a desire to kill the Lord Keeper, one of the wittnesse agaynst him was Sir William Clifton his brother, the Warden of the Fleet, with others, wherevppon he was by the Lords of the Councell committed to the Tower of London.

[a] Prince Charles Lewis, born 22 Dec. 1617. In consequence of the death of his elder brother Prince Henry, who was drowned in 1629, he became, upon the death of his father in 1632, the representative of his family, but did not succeed to the Electorate until 1650. Died 1680.

[b] Gervase Clifton, first Baron Clifton.

The Emperour's ambassador, which was stayed (as is formerlye sayed) by the Bassa of Buda, and the Grand Signor's ambassador, which was stayed att Vienna, are on ether part sett att libertie.

The Prince of Poland is now in Moscovie, in the towne of Troecobutz; 2,000. gentlemen of Russia did there sweare homadge and fealtie vnto him; the inhabitants of the castell and towne of Winena hathe done the like; and in the opinion of most men itt is thought thatt the Prince,without great difficultie will obtayne that sovereigntie.

It is thought thatt the Turkes will denounce warre agaynst the Kinge of Pole for favoringe of the Cossackes.

Foscarini, who was the ambassador of Venice here when you departed England, is delayed still prisoner by the State, and his secretarye put into the gallies.

The siedge of Riga yett continews.

The Electors of Rhyne and Brandenburge have latelye bene att Dresden with the Elector of Saxe; they were no lesse magnificently receved then the Emperor and the Kinge of Bohemia were att there beinge with him; there busines was about the deferringe of the election of a Kinge of the Romanes vntill all the grievances of the empire be composed, which will receve a longe dispute, and itt is sayed thatt the Duke of Saxe or the Palatine will pretend vnto itt, and an vnion is labored betwene the Protestants and the Lutherans. The Emperor sent the Count of Zolleren ᵃ to oppose there assemblye butt itt prevayled little.

The Kinge of Spayne hathe latelye sent to Dunkerke two barques loaden with silver buillon to beate into money for the payment of the Archduke's armye, and to provide necessaries for the warre as occasion shall be offred.

The marriage intended betwene the Lantzgrave of Hesses daughter is supposed will vanishe in smoake.

ᵃ John George Count of Hohen-zollern. He was made a Prince of the Empire by the Emperor Ferdinand II. 1623, but died immediately afterwards.

CAMD. SOC.   T

Januarye.—The 1. day of this monethe the Kinge created the Erle of Buckingham Marques of Buckingham.

The 3. Mrs. Middlemore, the Mayde of Honnour,[a] died att Whithall.

The 7. Sir Francis Bacon, the Lord Keeper, was at Whitehall sworne Lord Chaunceler of England.

The 8. Sir Robert Naunton, one of the Masters of the Requests, was sworne principall Secretarye.

The 11. Sir Rallphe Freeman was sworne a Master of the Requests.

The same day Capten John Baylie, who came from Sir Wallter Raleghe at the Iland of Lanzarote, was from the councell table committed prisoner to the Gatehouse in Westminster.

The late peace made betwene Spayne and Savoy is like to breake out into new flames. On the Kinge of Spaynes part there is no perfourmance. Instead of renderinge of Vercelli, itt is newlye renforced and fortified, and so are all the other places which the Spaniards had possest themselves of.

The Governour of Millan, Don Pedro de Toledo, is to be shortlye recalled, and the Conde de Lemos to succeed him.

Part of the levies which the Counte de Levensteyne (so often before mentioned) are safelye arrived at Venice, and the remaynder is daylie expected.

The Venetians are out of all hope to accord ether with the Kinges of Bohemia or Spayne; they prepare for the continuance of the warre, and by there ambassadors they have sollicited the Kinge our master, the Kinge of France, and Vnited Provinces, thatt for there money they may hir[e soldiers] to serve them, which is granted by our soveragne, with this cavtion, thatt they shallbe employed for defence onelye.

The Kinge of Poland hathe made himsellfe master of all Curland, the towne of Pernav excepted.

The Kinge of Sweden still continewes his siedge before Riga.

[a] Mrs. Middlemore was Maid of Honour 1603.

The 20. of December there passed throughe Dvysborg an Extraordinarye Ambassador frome the Kinge of Spayne to the Kinge of Denmarke, and, as itt is sayed, thatt he is to present him with the order of the Toyson.

Five shippes of Amsterdame richlye laden, in passinge the Strayghts homewarde bounde, are taken by the Turkishe piratts, and allso another of the same towne, very riche, bound for Venice.

At this present the Vnited Provinces have 18. good shippes of warre in the Mediterran Sea.

There is now 40. sayle of Turkishe pirattts gone past the Straytes to robbe and spoyle the Canaries, or the Azores, or bothe, and the Duke of Florence hathe latelye taken 2. of those piratts, and hathe made 240. of there men slaves.

Beinge now advertised by Sir Thomas Smythe thatt the shippes are readye to fall downe I am enforced to end this longe and tedious gazette.

I will not sweare thatt all which I have written is trew, but you may well beleeve thatt I have coyned nothinge. By the tyme thatt these shall come to your handes, I do hope thatt you will be readye to prepare your sellfe for England, where vuto I pray God you may safelye arrive, thatt once agayne your companie and conversion (*sic*) may be enioyed by

Your most affectionatt frend thatt loves you,

G. CAREW.

Savoy, this 18. of January, 1617.

At your retourne I do pray your Lordship to render vuto me all my gazetts, or ells thatt you would burne theme all att your departure from Svratte.

APPENDIX.

No. I.

Black Oliver St. John (p. 11)

THE identity of this person is involved in obscurity. We know but little relating to him. The proceedings on his trial are not recorded, with the exception of the speech of Lord Bacon on the prosecution, which is printed in Howell's State Trials, ii. 899, wherein he describes him as a gentleman of ancient house and name, and as being a principal person and a dweller in that town (Marlborough), and one whom the mayor considered likely to give both money and good example.

Lord Campbell supposes him to be the same Oliver St. John who in the reign of Charles I. was one of the prominent leaders of the republican party in the House of Commons, and who, in 1640, was made Solicitor-General and afterwards Lord Chief Justice. Clarendon states of the latter (book iii. 186) that he " was a lawyer of Lincoln's Inn, reserved and of a dark and clouded countenance,* very proud, and conversing with very few, and those men of his own humour and inclinations. He had been questioned, committed, and brought into the Star Chamber many years before, with other persons of great name and reputation (which first brought his name on the stage), for communicating some paper among themselves, which some men at that time had a mind to have extended to a design of sedition, but, it being quickly evident that the prosecution would not be attended with success, they were all shortly after discharged."

Lord Campbell was probably misled by the close similarity of the character, as here given, of St. John, the future Lord Chief Justice, to that of the gentleman mentioned in the text, although the historical part of the narrative does

---

* A swarthy complexion seems to have been hereditary in this family. Leland, Itinerary, vi. 27, speaking of " Olyver Saynt John, sonne to the excellent duchesse of Somerset" (as he is designated in his will, printed in Nicolas's Testamenta Vetusta, and in Jacob's Peerage, and which will is dated in 1496), describes him as " a blak and big felow that died at Fonterabye in Spayne, when the late Marquise of Dorset was there." This Oliver was the founder of the family of Lydiard Tregoze.

not agree with the case of the latter, in which the prosecution was quite successful. Mr. Foss, however, clearly proves his Lordship to be mistaken, by showing that the Oliver St. John who became Lord Chief Justice was born about the year 1598, and that he was admitted a pensioner of Queen's College, Cambridge, on Aug. 16, 1615, being then seventeen years of age. It is highly improbable that the letter to the Mayor of Marlborough * was written by such a youth, or that the prosecution of a mere boy would have created such anxiety at court as to cause, at the request of the Council,† the trial to be deferred until the Lord Chancellor (Egerton), who from age and infirmity was upon the point of resigning the great seal, could attend the hearing, "so necessary" did they "judg his presence there." The statement of Mr. Foss is confirmed by the will of Oliver St. John of Cayshoe, co. Beds, which proves the parentage of the Lord Chief Justice, and shows that in 1625 he was still a student in London. Mr. Foss falls into a still more remarkable error himself by stating, upon the authority of Harris's Lives, that Black Oliver mentioned in the text was Oliver St. John of Lydiard Tregoze, who in 1622 was created Lord Grandison. The printed genealogical accounts which we have of this gentleman certainly state that in his youth "he was sent to study the law in the Inns of Court, but having been engaged in a duel he was obliged to quit the kingdom." He served in the Low Countries under the Veres, and *was knighted in the reign of Queen Elizabeth.* He afterwards distinguished himself in the wars in Ireland, and in December 1605 was made Master of the Ordnance in that kingdom, which office he continued to hold until 1616. He thus spent the early part of the reign of James I. in that country, and we find him taking an active part in the debates in the Irish House of Commons in 1613 and 1614. In 1615 he seems to have been in England, but not in disgrace, for in October of that year he was so much in the confidence of the King as to be entrusted with the custody of the Earl of Somerset, and in the following April he was appointed Lord Deputy of Ireland. He could not, therefore, be the same person who was prosecuted and received so severe a sentence in April 1615, as *Mr.* St. John of Marlborough, who is no-where spoken of as a Knight.

Having disposed of the claims advanced for these two gentlemen, it remains to be considered who was " Black Oliver St. John," who on 11 October, 1614, wrote the letter to the Mayor of Marlborough. Chamberlain calls him " Oliver St. John of Wiltshire." He was therefore in all probability of the Lydiard stock, and, on turning to the pedigree of that branch of St. John, recorded in the Heralds' College, we find that John St. John of Lydiard had two sons,

* The original letter, written in a legal hand, is in the S. P. O. vol. lxxviii. 23.
† Privy Council Register.—S. P. O. Dom. Corr. James I. vol. lxxx. 24.

John, the grandfather of Oliver who became Lord Grandison, and Oliver, who had a son of his own name, described as "son and heir."

The elder Oliver is stated by Edmonson, iv. 328, to have married Margaret, daughter and coheir of —— Love, of Winchelsea, and to have had three sons: Oliver, Nicholas, and John. This statement is confirmed by the following document among the title-deeds of an estate called Troppinden, in Sussex, preserved among the Evidences of George E. Courthope, of Whilegh, in that county, Esq. by whom it has been kindly communicated.

" Sir Edward Randyll, Knt. and Dame Anne his wife, by Ind're 10 May, 6 Jas. did sell unto Thomas Risly of Brenchley the moiety of all these lands and tenements.

[The preamble of the said Indenture is as follows: Between Sir Edward Randill, of Albury, co. Surry, Knt. and dame Anne his wife, sole dau'r and heir of Anne Morgan, dec[d], late wife of Sir John Morgan, Knt. and one of the dau's and heirs of John Love, late of Winchelsey, co. Sussex, Gent.]

" Olyver St.John, Esq. by Ind're same date, did sell the other moiety to said Thomas Risley.

[The preamble of the said Indenture is as follows: Nicholas St.John, Gent. one of the sons of Olyver St.John, Esq. and of Margaret his wife, one of the dau'rs of John Love, dec[d], late of Winchelsey, Merchant.]

" Thomas Risly, by will, 6 Feb. 1612, gives all s[d] lands to Symon Bynyor, who sold the same to Stephen Ballard and Richard Besbeech.

" Richard Besbeech hath the custody of all the ancient writings.

" John Love,[*] of Winchelsey, dee[d], was owner of these premises, and he had issue 2 dau'rs, viz[t]. Margaret, who married to the said Oliver St.John, and another to Sir John Morgan, Knt. and died leaving issue only the said Ann, wife of the af[d] Sir Edward Randyll.

" Margaret died leaving issue Nicholas St.John, Oliver St.John, and John St. John, for whom their father hath undertaken that they shall release, or else there is a lease for 1000 y'rs for security.

" Nicholas St. John hath already released.

" The other two brothers be not of age.[†]

                                        " RICHARD BESBEECH."

---

[*] He made his will, dated 26 Mar. 1593; names "son St. John and Margaret my dau'r his wife, all lands, &c."—"son St. John, house he now lives in in Winchilsea—" son Morgan, house in Winchilsea," &c. After his decease to " Anne Morgan, his dau'r begotten on Anne Love deceased, late dau'r of me the said John Love."

[†] A subsequent Indenture, dated 5 May, 13 Jas. (1615), shows that Oliver and John St. John were still under age, and that their father Oliver was living at Marlborough, co. Wilts, and their mother was dead.

It appears from this document that Oliver St.John and Margaret Love were married before 1593, when John Love made his will, in all probability just previous to that date, for in 1612 Oliver St.John's eldest son was of age, and the two younger were yet minors in 1615. In 1593 he resided at Winchelsea. How soon afterwards he settled at Marlborough we have no evidence to show, but we find his name, as an inhabitant of that town, in an armoury book preserved in the corporation chest of the date of 1606 ; and the register of burials of the parish of St. Mary shows that—

" Margaret, wife of Oliver St.John, gent. (was) buried Sept. 19th, 1606."

This entry agrees with the statement in the Indenture of 5 May, 13 Jas. that the mother of his three sons was dead. After the death of this wife he seems to have re-married, for the register above quoted records that—

" Mrs. St.John, wife of Mr. Oliver St.John (was) buried April 3rd, 1608."

In the "Taxation of the Freeholders of the Borough, and Out-dwellers holding freeholds, for aid-money to marry the Princess Elizabeth," his name does not appear. This, however, was the benevolence against which he wrote, and as it was regarded as a free gift, the names of the contributors, only, would be recorded. The above document shows that he was a resident in Marlborough in 1615. We have no evidence of the date when he died, but the will of an Oliver St.John is recorded in the registers of the Prerogative Court of Canterbury in the year 1639, although, unfortunately, as stated in a marginal note in the volume, neither the original nor any copy can be found. No trace of his burial is found in the Marlborough registers.

If, therefore, we can regard Edmonson as correct in stating that Oliver, the second son of John St.John of Lydiard, was the husband of the daughter of —— Love, of Winchelsea, there can be no reasonable cause to doubt his identity with "Black Oliver." Only one discrepancy remains to be disposed of. Both Edmonson and the Visitation Pedigree of 1623 show Oliver as the " son and heir" of Oliver St.John, by Margaret Love. This can only be reconciled by supposing that Nicholas, who is proved by the above document to have been his eldest son, died between 1612, when he released his interest in Troppinden, and 1623.

No. II.

The goodlye mannour of Shirborne (p 48)

Chamberlain says that Sherborne was at first given to Villiers, but he resigned it. " In the meanwhile it is bestowed upon Sir John Digby, which, besides the goodly house and other commodities, is presently worth 800*l.* a year, and in reasonable time will be double. I cannot yet learn how or why this good fortune is befallen him, but sure it is somewhat extraordinary." (Birch, i. 426.) Castle says that " Villiers refused it in a most noble fashion, praying the King that the building of his fortunes may not be founded upon the ruins of another."

This disinterestedness on the part of a royal favourite is somewhat remarkable, and was not manifested by Villiers in his other large acquisitions. We may, therefore, look for some other cause than that assigned, and such cause is probably shown by the following curious contemporary document preserved in the State Paper Office, and recently printed by Mr. Noel Sainsbury in the Literary Gazette :—

" *An inevitable curse by a Norman bishopp to all succeeding times, as appeareth following :*

" ' Osmund,* a Norman knight, almost 600 yeares sithence, com'ing into this cuntrey wth Will'm the Conqueror, became afterwards Earle of Dorsett, and, being a godlie man, forsooke the earledome and became Bishopp of Salisburie, and gave the lands called Sherborne, thereto adioyning, to remaine to that sea for ever, wth addic'on of a curse to such as should take it from the b'ppricke in greate or small things, not onlie in this world, but in the world to come, unless he made restitution in his life time.

" ' This Osmund was afterwards canonized a saint, and it happened afterwards that King Stephen tooke from a B'pp of the same sea, called Roger the Riche, the said lands, who after, during his life, had but a troublesome raigne ; another being his competitor in the kingdome, who at length succeeded him in the whole, had those lands, but enioyed them not longe.

" ' Theis lands afterwards came to the possession of the house of the Mountagues, Earles of Salisburie, whereof one was slaine, being defending Towers in Fraunce ; another alsoe was taken prisoner there ; and then another bishopp, called Robt Wymell, brought a writt of right ag^t Will'm Montague, Earl of

* Osmund de Seez died 1099.

Salisburie, for theis lands; the trial being by combate, and the champions readie to fight, the King E. 3 tooke up the quarrell for 2000 mks., and soe the b'pp had theis lands againe, and there they rested vntill E. 6 time, when the Duke of Som'sett had these lands, and he noe sooner gott them but hee fell, and afterwards lost his head.

"'Afterwards B'pp Capon* exhibited a bill in Chancerie, p'tending the Duke, as Protector, had gotten the lands from him by threats; and thereupon, by decree in Chancerie, they came back againe to the B'ppricke.

"'And in 34 Eliz. Sr Walter Raleigh gott theis lands, who p'sentlie after fell into her Ma^{ts} dislike, and afterwards hee fell from that to what he now is; then Prince Henry gott them, but enioyed them but a small time, to the great grief of all the world that lost him soe soon.

"'And now lastlie, the Earl of Somersett hadd those lands, whose fall is much feared to be greate.'"

Sir John Digby was not more fortunate than his predecessors in the posses-sion of this estate. At the time he received it he stood high in the favour of his sovereign, who showered upon him numerous honours; but within a very short time he was crushed by his rival Buckingham, and cast into prison. After his release he lived in seclusion until the commencement of the troubles of the succeeding reign. At first he put himself forward as a leader of the popular party, but deserting that cause, and adhering to the King, he incurred their implacable hatred. He was obliged to retire into France; all his pro-perty was seized by the Parliament, for which he was not permitted, like other Royalists, to compound. He died in exile 16 Jan. 1652-3, and was succeeded by his son George, K.G. who had been summoned to parliament in his father's lifetime by writ as Baron Digby, 9 June, 1641; and he, upon the restoration of Charles II., received back his estates, but, having changed his religion whilst abroad, was incapable of holding any office. He died 20 March, 1676, leaving one surviving son, who succeeded him as third Earl of Bristol, but died 1698 without issue, when all his honours became extinct. The manor now devolved upon William fifth Lord Digby in the Irish peerage. But the curse seems still to cling to it. This nobleman had five sons and seven daughters. His three eldest sons and four daughters died unmarried, and his fourth son died during his father's life. Lord Digby died Nov. 1752, and was succeeded by his grandson, Edward, eldest son of his fourth son. Edward died unmarried 27 Nov. 1757, and was succeeded by his brother Henry, created Earl Digby and Viscount Coleshill. Henry was twice married. By his first wife he had an only child Edward, who died in infancy. By his second wife he had four

---

* John Salcot, or Capon, 1539—59.

sons and two daughters, of whom one son and one daughter died young, and another son without issue. He died 25 Sept. 1793, and was succeeded by his son Edward, second Earl, who died unmarried 11 May, 1856, when the diguities of Earl Digby and Viscount Coleshill became extinct; but he was suc. ceeded in the title of Baron Digby of Sherborne in the peerage of Great Britain, created in 1765, by his cousin the present Lord Digby.

INDEX.

X

Westminster: Printed by J. B. Nichols and Sons, 25, Parliament Street.

Lightning Source UK Ltd.
Milton Keynes UK
UKOW01f0939180717
305535UK00001B/33/P